NAGARJUNA'S *Letter to a Friend*

WITH COMMENTARY BY KANGYUR RINPOCHE

Buddha Shakyamuni

༄༅། །སློབ་དཔོན་འཕགས་པ་ཀླུ་སྒྲུབ་ཀྱི་བཤེས་པའི་སྤྲིང་ཡིག་གི་མཆན་འགྲེལ་ཞལ་རྒྱུན་བདུད་རྩིའི་ཐིགས་མ་སྐྱབས་རྗེ་བཀའ་འགྱུར་རིན་པོ་ཆེའི་གསུང་། །

པདྨ་ཀཱ་རའི་སྒྲ་བསྒྱུར་མཐུན་ཚོགས་ནས་
སྒྲ་བསྒྱུར་ཞུས།།

The Padmakara Translation Group gratefully acknowledges the generous support of the Tsadra Foundation in sponsoring the translation and preparation of this book.

NAGARJUNA'S *Letter to a Friend*

WITH COMMENTARY BY KANGYUR RINPOCHE

LETTER TO A FRIEND
by Nagarjuna • The Root Text

THE NECTAR-LIKE WORDS OF THE TEACHER
by Longchen Yeshe Dorje, Kangyur Rinpoche • The Commentary

Translated by the Padmakara Translation Group

SNOW LION PUBLICATIONS
ITHACA, NEW YORK • BOULDER, COLORADO

Snow Lion Publications
P. O. Box 6483
Ithaca, NY 14851 USA
(607) 273-8519
www.snowlionpub.com

Drawing of Nagarjuna by Olivier Philippot
Photograph of Kangyur Rinpoche by Matthieu Ricard
Text designed and typeset by Gopa & Ted2, Inc.

Printed in U.S.A. on acid-free recycled paper.
ISBN-10 1-55939-227-4
ISBN-13 978-1-55939-227-3

Library of Congress Cataloging-in-Publication Data

Klong-chen Ye-shes-rdo-rje, Bka'-'gyur Rin-po-che
[Slob-dpon 'phags pa Klu-sgrub kyi Bśes pa'i spriṅ yig gi mchan 'grel źal rgyun bdud rtsi'i zegs ma skyabs rje bka' 'gyur rin po che'i gsuṅ. English]
Nagarjuna's letter to a friend, with commentary by Kangyur Rinpoche / translated by the Padmakara Translation Group.
p. cm.
Root text: Suhṛllekha (in Sanskrit); commentary: Slob dpon 'phags pa klu sgrub kyi bśes pa'i spriṅ yig gi mchan 'grel źal rgyun bdud rtsi'i zegs ma skyabs rje bka' 'gyur rin po che'i gsuṅ (in Tibetan).
Includes bibliographical references and index.
Contents: Letter to a friend by Nagarjuna (the root text) — The nectar-like words of the teacher by Longchen Yeshe Dorje, Kangyur Rinpoche (the commentary)
ISBN-13: 978-1-55939-227-3 (alk. paper)
ISBN-10: 1-55939-227-4 (alk. paper)
1. Nāgārjuna, 2nd cent. Suhṛllekha. 2. Religious life—Mahayana Buddhism. 3. Buddhism —Doctrines. 4. Priests, Buddhist—India—Correspondence. I. Nāgārjuna, 2nd cent. Suhṛllekha. English. II. Title.
BQ5385.N333K56 2005
294.3'444—dc22

2005012500

Contents

Foreword

THE GREAT INDIAN MASTER Arya Nagarjuna was remarkable for his ability to condense the whole of the Buddha's teachings into comprehensive works without in any way diluting them. As predicted by Shakyamuni Buddha himself, he is especially noted for having expounded the profound meanings of the doctrine.

The work presented in this book is a letter that he wrote to his friend and student King Dechö Zangpo (as he is known in Tibetan), and as such it provides a frank yet subtly pointed exposition of the entire Buddhist path, from the basic foundations of discipline to the profundities of the Mahayana view. It is addressed to anyone, whether an ordained monk or nun or a lay person, who sincerely wishes to practice the Buddha's teaching as a means to become free from samsara.

If Nagarjuna's approach in his *Letter to a Friend* sometimes does not appear to entertain us, we should understand that he is, in a clear and unadorned manner, showing us the path to liberation, not writing a novel. His aim is not to seek fame as a best-selling author, but to benefit his friend and anyone else willing to respond to the honest advice he gives.

I am happy that Nagarjuna's message, complemented by Kangyur Rinpoche's commentary, is being made available for English readers seeking an authentic spiritual path.

Jigme Khyentse
Dordogne, 2005

Translator's Introduction

FEW PEOPLE who have begun studying Tibetan Buddhism can remain unaware for long of the importance of Nagarjuna's *Letter to a Friend* (*Suhrillekha* in Sanskrit), for even if they have not had the opportunity to read it on its own, they will sooner or later come across quotations from Nagarjuna's poem in the many written and oral commentaries on other texts that the Tibetan tradition has produced. The *Letter to a Friend,* despite its short length, is a monument of the Indian shastra tradition, for it covers the whole Mahayana path with unusual clarity and memorable imagery. For many students of Buddhism the original canonical texts—that is, the sutras and other works that recorded the Buddha's teachings and were translated in the Tibetan Kangyur—could prove somewhat daunting, for there is a vast number of them and they often confine themselves to specific subjects, being in most cases delivered in response to specific situations. To gain an overall perspective of the whole Buddhist path required not only an exceptional memory but also a formidable ability to order and synthesize the material expressed in the sutras. It was to enable students to better grasp the real message of the whole scope and variety of the Buddha's teachings that, centuries after the Buddha had left this world, Indian masters like Nagarjuna composed the many shastras of the later canonical tradition that were translated in the Tibetan Tengyur. To think of the shastras simply as commentaries is not always entirely meaningful, for such works as the *Letter to a Friend* and Shantideva's *The Way of the Bodhisattva* condense rather than expand on the Buddha's original teachings. They are, all the same, entirely based on the Buddha's words, and indeed many lines in the *Letter to a Friend* specifically refer to passages in the sutras. These references serve as keys to jog the reader's memory, though they assume, of course, that the reader is already familiar with these same sutras. A glance at the last two lines of verse 68, and at the corresponding section in the commentary with its quotation from the sutra alluded to, provides a good illustration of this. It also shows why it has been necessary for subsequent masters, both in India and Tibet, to in their turn compose commentaries that explain and expand on these shastras. Works like the *Letter to a Friend*, which could be easily memorized, thus provided a framework on which the Buddhist practitioner could "hang" the detailed expositions to be found in the sutras. And, since they covered a wide range of topics, they were useful as scriptural sources to be quoted by Tibetan writers explaining specific points of the Buddhist teachings.

Nagarjuna

Nagarjuna is generally considered with Asanga to be the most important figure in Mahayana Buddhism. Acknowledged as the father of Madhyamika, it was he who brought to the human world the *Prajñaparamita in One Hundred Thousand Verses* (hitherto hidden in the realm of the nagas) which inspired his own *Mulamadhyamaka-karika*, on which the entire Madhyamika is based. A prolific writer, his works include the *Six Texts on Reasoning*, hymns of praise, and a number of discourses (including the *Letter to a Friend*). As principal abbot of Nalanda he was largely responsible for increasing this great monastic university's reputation as a seat of learning and pure conduct. Most of the details of his life, however, have come down to us largely in the form of legend, and as with many great masters of the first few hundred years after the Buddha's parinirvana, it is difficult to form a clear picture from all the numerous and varied accounts available. The Buddha himself predicted that Nagarjuna would be born four hundred years after his own parinirvana, and that he would live six hundred years. This in fact correlates with the dates most scholars attribute for him, which lie somewhere around the first and second centuries of the Christian era, falling roughly in the middle of the period foretold by the Buddha.

Despite this prediction of longevity, it seemed at first that Nagarjuna's life would be a short one. A soothsayer consulted soon after his birth told his parents that the baby would only survive seven days unless they were to make offerings to one hundred monks, which condition they were only too happy to fulfill. But having been told subsequently that nothing could be done to extend the boy's life longer than seven years, they sent him away shortly before his seventh birthday so that they would not have to endure the sorrow of seeing their son's corpse. It was as a result of his arrival at Nalanda, where he was ordained and initiated into a tantric practice conferring immortality by the great master Saraha (also known in this context as Rahulabhadra), that he not only survived this second deadline but went on to become a learned scholar and fully accomplished practitioner, mastering the teachings of the sutras and tantras, and even the science of alchemy. Throughout his life he significantly benefited the doctrine and sentient beings, on many occasions using miraculous powers. The special relationship he cultivated with the nagas, and which enabled him to retrieve the *Prajñaparamita in One Hundred Thousand Verses*, is reflected not only in his name but in numerous representations of him depicting the nagas' cobralike heads shading him from the sun as he taught the Dharma.

King Surabhibhadra

While contemporary Sanskrit sources have provided modern scholars with some idea of Nagarjuna's life, it is impossible to identify the friend for whom he wrote his *Letter* because no Sanskrit version of this work has survived. His original name can only be surmised by translating back into Sanskrit the two Tibetan names that exist in different versions of the text. As a result, we find him variously referred to in different translations of the *Letter* as Surabhibhadra (the name we have adopted here, albeit arbitrarily), Udayibhadra, Udayana, Gautamiputra, Kanishka, Shatavahana, and so on. All we can say is that he was probably one of a number of Andhran kings ruling in Central India at the time Nagarjuna lived there. Nonetheless, even if a knowledge of the historical background to a work of literature can sometimes give valuable insights into the text itself, in this case precise identification of the king is not crucial to understanding Nagarjuna's message and does not affect its value as a basis for Buddhist practice.

Letter to a Friend

The *Letter to a Friend* is unusual in that it covers the entire Mahayana path in no more than 123 verses, and it is hardly surprising that many passages need a certain amount of explanation if they are to be properly understood. A number of commentaries were written on it in Tibet, of which two, one by the Nyingmapa Lama Mipham (1846-1912) and the other by the fourteenth-century Sakya master Jetsun Rendawa, have been translated into English. The present translation is of a commentary by Kyabje Kangyur Rinpoche, and is a further tribute to him as the founding father and abiding inspiration of the Padmakara Translation Group, which has already translated his commentary on Jigme Lingpa's *Treasury of Precious Qualities*.

Kyabje Kangyur Rinpoche (1897-1975)

Kangyur Rinpoche, Longchen Yeshe Dorje, was born in Eastern Tibet and began studying the Dharma and practicing from an early age. His root guru was Jedrung Rinpoche, Trinle Jampa Jungne, of Riwoche Monastery, famous for its nonsectarian approach and its annual festival in which its two main colleges, one Nyingmapa and the other belonging to the Taklung Kagyu tradition, used to practice together. His former life as Namkhai Nyingpo, one of Guru Padmasambhava's twenty-five closest disciples, became evident in the revealing of teachings he had received and hidden during that time and which in this life he rediscovered as spiritual treasures (*terma*).

Kangyur Rinpoche's life broadly falls into two periods. The first half of his life, in fulfillment of his teachers' wishes, he devoted to study and practice. After receiving the empowerment of Mañjushri from Mipham Rinpoche, he was able to memorize any text at a single reading. His diligence in study was unmatched, and he would read far into the night, his only source of light the glowing tip of an incense stick on which he blew from time to time to make it brighter. In this way he became extraordinarily learned, not only in the whole range of subjects taught in the different schools of Tibetan Buddhism, but in a wide variety of practical subjects as well. At the same time, he combined perfect observance of his monastic vows (his only possessions were his monk's robes) with a number of long retreats, thus adding profound meditational experience and accomplishment to his immense scholarship. He was thus able to contribute in no small measure to all aspects of the life of Riwoche Monastery and eventually held the most important posts there.

His disregard for status of any sort led to his abandoning his position in the monastery and taking to the life of a wandering hermit. Although he never ceased to study and practice, this second period of his life was characterized by his extraordinary humanity and his work in helping others, in particular the four activities he cherished most—caring for the chronically ill (he was a skilled doctor), looking after the aged, helping travellers, and caring for orphans—and his work in preserving and spreading the teachings. The latter included not only the numerous occasions on which he transmitted the teachings—he was named Kangyur Rinpoche for his having given the reading transmission of the hundred or so volumes that make up the Tibetan Kangyur no fewer than twenty-four times—but also the important work of restoring monasteries and stupas. It is a measure of his deep humility that in these and other projects his role was by no means confined to organizing, funding, and providing inspiration, for he took an active part in them and surprised many by displaying unexpected talents, doing the work of a mason, for example, as if he had exercised that particular trade all his life.

The preservation of the Dharma became Kangyur Rinpoche's principal concern in the last twenty years of his life as he realized the future of Buddhism in Tibet was threatened. He and his family brought to India many rare books that might otherwise have been lost, and in India he took every opportunity to ensure that the Buddha's teachings were transmitted to the next generation, eventually founding a monastery in Darjeeling where Tibetan children could be given a traditional education from an early age. Although he never fulfilled his expressed wish to visit Europe or America, it was clearly important to him that the Dharma should become established in the West. He gave unsparingly of his time to Westerners who came to see him, and a number of them spent many months practicing under his guidance. Due to his personal requests to other great masters, among them Dilgo Khyentse Rinpoche and Dudjom Rinpoche, and also as a result of his inspiration in the activities of his sons Taklung Tsetrul Pema Wangyal Rinpoche, Jigme Khyentse Rinpoche, and Rangdrol Rinpoche, many Westerners have now been able to study and practice the Dharma, some of them in the context of the traditional three-year retreat.

The Commentary

Kangyur Rinpoche's commentary broadly serves three purposes. First of all it provides a structural outline (*sa bcad*) for Nagarjuna's text, furnishing appropriate headings with each change in topic; effectively this occurs almost with each new verse. On a casual reading of the root text, it is by no means easy to follow Nagarjuna's argument and a structural outline is essential if readers are to have an overview of the entire work and keep their bearings as they read. Texts of this kind are open to more than a single interpretation and it is therefore possible to have more than one structural outline, which is indeed the case for *Letter to a Friend.* Jetsun Rendawa's outline, for example, divides the text into three main sections: general advice concerning virtuous practices, developing aversion to samsara, and pursuing the path to nirvana. Sakya Pandita's outline views the *Letter to a Friend* more in terms of how it presents the Three Trainings, while the commentary by the Gelugpa Geshe Lobsang Jinba divides the text into practices for the three kinds of beings.[1] Kangyur Rinpoche's outline puts the emphasis on the six transcendent perfections, and in this respect it is very similar to the outline that determines Lama Mipham's commentary.

Secondly, the commentary furnishes explanations on the more difficult points in Nagarjuna's poem by the insertion of notes between the words of the root text. These notes vary in their scope and purpose. Some constitute the simple insertion of synonyms to provide clarification of ambiguous words or modern equivalents for anachronistic expressions. Other notes explain what Nagarjuna means by particular terms. In some cases, Kangyur Rinpoche inserts quotations from the sutras and shastras, and for a number of topics he has written entire pages of detailed commentary.

The third purpose of Kangyur Rinpoche's commentary is to render the original, sometimes cryptic, verse into relatively straightforward prose. While it would have been interesting to have reproduced the commentary in English exactly as it is in the Tibetan, the structural differences between the two languages make this almost impossible without the result appearing stilted and difficult to read. We have therefore approached the task of translation more with the authors' original intentions in mind. Our aim has been, on the one hand, to render Kangyur Rinpoche's annotated version as prose that, even if occasionally cumbersome on account of the density of ideas it contains, can be understood without great difficulty by practicing Buddhists; and on the other hand, to attempt to use the expressive powers of language to emulate Nagarjuna's original poem and present his message in a form that is at once inspiring and memorable.

The requirements of meter and rhythm for the latter have involved certain choices and shortcuts regarding vocabulary. While we have attempted to maintain accuracy and consistency in the translation of the commentary, some divergence and approximation have proved necessary in translating the poem. Thus "positive action" has often been rendered as "virtue" or simply "good," while for "negative actions" we have reverted to "evil deeds" and, with some reluctance, "sin." In some instances, however, we have used different equivalents in the commentary and poem for the sake of richness and to indicate a greater range of meaning than might otherwise have been conveyed with a strictly consistent use of vocabulary. Words from the root text have been highlighted in the commentary (as they are in the Tibetan) to indicate the correspondence with the root text, but, for the reasons just given, they do not necessarily appear in the same order and are in some cases synonyms or equivalents of the words to be found in the translated root text.

Not everyone will find our imperfect attempt at rendering the translation of Nagarjuna's text as poetry entirely to their taste. Some will argue that certain verses require too great an effort to be understood. While we have tried to make the translation as clear and readable as possible, we have, wherever possible, avoided adding anything that is not Nagarjuna's. In taking a traditional view that it is the function of the commentary, not of the translators, to explain the text, we hope that, where readers encounter passages in the root text that seem difficult or even incomprehensible, they will seek clarification in the relevant sections of the commentary. We would also suggest that reading the poem aloud may resolve certain difficulties.

Brief Overview

Given that Nagarjuna's poem condenses the entire Bodhisattva path into 123 four-line verses, with a structural outline running to several pages and going some twenty levels deep, it is not always easy to keep track of the direction the text is taking. The following general overview may therefore prove helpful, particularly for those unfamiliar with the classical structural outline.

As is traditional with Indian shastras, the author begins with a commitment to compose the text, followed by encouragement to the reader on how to approach the text properly. He then introduces the principal subject of his poem, the Bodhisattva path. He starts with a brief reminder (verses 4 to 7) of six subjects (common to all the Buddhist vehicles) that one needs to keep in mind in order to inspire faith: the Three Jewels, the value of positive actions, generosity, and discipline. Nagarjuna then loses no time in moving onto his main subject, the six transcendent perfections (Skt. *paramitas*), which makes up the bulk of the poem. The first four perfections (generosity, discipline, patience, and diligence) are dealt with only briefly in the next eleven verses, and it is only the last two, concentration and wisdom, that Nagarjuna discusses in any detail.

Concentration (verses 21-44), according to Nagarjuna, requires careful preparation and implies assiduously avoiding distraction. To this he allots some nineteen verses, emphasizing the dangers of worldly preoccupations, including sexual desire. A final verse on the preparation for concentration is dedicated to the four boundless thoughts (love, compassion, and so on). The actual practice of concentration is dealt with in a single verse, which provides an outline of the four concentrations (Skt. *samadhis*). This section concludes with three verses that discuss the postmeditational practice in as far as concentration is concerned, in particular the factors that can hinder one's concentration.

Nagarjuna now comes to the heart of his subject, dedicating no less than seventy verses (45-115)—about half of the entire poem—to the perfection of wisdom. One might expect here that, as the father of Madhyamika, he would treat the reader to a debate establishing the Madhyamika view, much as does Shantideva in the ninth chapter of the *Bodhicharyavatara* or Chandrakirti in the *Madhyamakavatara*, but he has of course written elsewhere on this. In the *Letter to a Friend* Nagarjuna's discussion of the two truths consists mainly of an extensive analysis of relative truth. After a preamble on the factors that favor the cultivation of wisdom, in which he briefly presents the path of joining and introduces us to the correct view, he touches on a presentation of the absolute truth, or emptiness, in verses 49 and 50 before proceeding to an explanation of the training in wisdom. It is at this point that readers accustomed to the graded approach of the *lam rim* teachings may feel slightly disorientated, for while those texts begin with basic subjects such as the rarity of the precious human body, impermanence, and the defects of samsara long before they make any mention of the transcendent perfection of wisdom, it is these "preliminaries" that

Nagarjuna now discusses at considerable length, devoting no fewer than fifty verses to them, and they form the first part of the training in wisdom. This is divided into two, a presentation in terms of this present life of impermanence (verses 55-58) and the rarity of human birth (59-64); and a detailed discussion, with a view to getting out of samsara completely, (a) of how nothing in samsara can be relied on (66-75) and (b) of the suffering in the different realms (77-102). Nagarjuna seems to want the reader to understand that it is in mastering these topics that the realization of Madhyamika will come naturally. Only then does he continue with the second part of the training which, in just eleven verses, covers the paths of seeing and meditation and includes an overview of the important subject of interdependence.

Nagarjuna rounds off this highly condensed description of the Bodhisattva path with three or four verses of encouragement, reassuring the king that the path, however difficult it may seem, is possible even for ordinary individuals. Stick to the essential, and do your best, he says, before concluding his poem with the traditional dedication of merit, in which he gives us a glimpse of the final result, Buddhahood.

Some people might reasonably wonder whether a classical text in the form of advice addressed to an Indian king living almost two thousand years ago has much relevance for members of Western society in the twenty-first century. And yet as we read the *Letter* it is worth asking ourselves what sort of person Nagarjuna's "friend" is. On the assumption that the author's advice was originally intended for King Surabhibhadra personally (along with his court, perhaps), and that he did not go out of his way to flatter him, we can glean a number of clues as to the king's character from the text itself. Despite leading a busy court life with the usual responsibilities of royalty, he appears already to have a good knowledge of the Buddha's teachings (verse 3), and Nagarjuna makes frequent allusions to passages in the sutras, which must assume more than a passing acquaintance with the latter. The manner in which Nagarjuna addresses him would suggest that the king is essentially a good and indeed devout man, though at the same time prone to distraction and easily enticed by the pleasures of court life. Nagarjuna evidently feels it necessary to warn him to keep a roving eye off other people's wives (verse 21) and, as for the king's own marriage, Nagarjuna clearly considers it important to give him some advice on the matter and devotes no less than two verses to this. Nor does he allow the king a few mild fantasies as to the life he can expect in the celestial realms as a reward for suitable behavior in the present life, but reminds him that even the greatest happiness that might result from positive deeds is bound to end (verse 70 et seq.). Elsewhere (verse 33, for example) Nagarjuna advises the king against other temptations to which it seems he might easily fall prey, and the admonition not to prowl around at night comes as something of a surprise if we are to take it as a reflection on the king's habits. Again, the essential advice on eating habits a few verses later would suggest that Surabhibhadra is something of a *bon vivant*. Yet when it comes to practicing the Buddhist path, he would seem to be prone to doubts, for shortly before concluding his letter Nagarjuna provides a few lines of reassurance: the great Bodhisattvas were all once perfectly ordinary people like you, he tells him, so you can be sure that you will get enlightened too.

If some of the above is speculative, it hopefully provides a picture of Nagarjuna's friend as an essentially human person, prone to the weaknesses and doubts that we all have in common. We may not be heads-of-state or wealthy aristocrats, but many Buddhists in the West do share with King Surabhibhadra a relatively comfortable background and lifestyle, and no shortage of worldly distractions. Seen in this light, Nagarjuna's advice is as valid and contemporary as it was when he wrote it. True, there are a number of points that have to be understood in their ancient Indian context and adapted accordingly. Not many Americans or Europeans are likely to find themselves tempted, for example, to commit negative actions for the sake of brahmins (verse 30), but it is nevertheless important not to fall under the misconception that to do something negative, thinking that it is for one's teacher's sake, lets one off the karmic hook. Similarly, the advice to reflect on women's bodies as being unclean has to be understood in its proper context as an important meditational device for remedying attachment, in this case addressed to a heterosexual layman but applicable, with an appropriate change in wording, to anyone for whom sexual desire is likely to prove a distraction from meditation. Far from being a misogynistic tirade, it is intended to make us take a cool, objective look at what it is that makes us slaves to our passions and thus see them for what they are with a little less frustration and even a certain sense of humor. Other passages that may seem difficult to relate to if taken at face value include the traditional descriptions of the different realms of samsara. Here it is important to understand that, according to Buddhist teachings, the six realms of samsara are all illusions, hallucinations perceived by the minds that have created them, and that the descriptions found in the texts are broad generalizations of an infinite number of such hallucinations that are possible. The hells are experiences of intense anger and fear arising from attitudes dominated by aversion and hatred. It is these very emotions that create the torment and confusion perceived, in its furious, extroverted form, as the hot hells, and in a more introverted form as the cold hells. The fate of the pretas in the realm of hungry ghosts reflects the attitudes, grossly magnified, of minds driven in earlier lives by intense desire and an inability to give anything away. And the fact that these states are generally associated with specific individual realms does not prevent them from being experienced less intensely in other realms. Who among us in the human realm has not experienced the paralyzing effect of cold hatred or the unbearable paranoia of jealousy, or observed the truth in the saying, "Pride comes before a fall"?

A work of this sort that covers such a wide range of subjects is bound to contain many unexplained technical points. We have done our best to provide short explanations of many of them by providing notes and a glossary of technical terms. Readers who wish to explore subjects in greater detail are invited to consult other larger works on the Mahayana path, in particular *Treasury of Precious Qualities*, in which Kangyur Rinpoche provides further commentary on many of the subjects treated here, Patrul Rinpoche's *The Words of My Perfect Teacher*, and other books mentioned in the Bibliography.

Acknowledgments

This book was inspired by Taklung Tsetrul Rinpoche, Pema Wangyal, who has devoted much effort to ensuring that the writings of Kangyur Rinpoche and other great masters are preserved in correct Tibetan editions and to seeing important Buddhist works made available in other languages. As well as according us the immense privilege of translating this commentary on the *Suhrillekha* into English and giving the oral transmission of this work, he and Jigme Khyentse Rinpoche spent many hours supervising the project and patiently clarifying numerous points of translation. No printed acknowledgment could hope to convey the debt of gratitude we owe them. We would also like to extend our thanks to Alak Zenkar Rinpoche, who as well as answering a number of questions kindly sent us a copy of another commentary for us to refer to, and to Khenpo Pema Sherab and Lobpon Nyima Dondrup for their advice on some difficult points.

The translation was made by Stephen Gethin with assistance from Wulstan Fletcher and Helena Blankleder, all of them members of the Padmakara Translation Group. Invaluable comments and suggestions were gratefully received from Barbara Gethin, Larry Gethin, Adrian Gunther, Geoff Gunther, Jennifer Kane, Durga Martin, Kali Martin, Bob Rickner, and Dave Smith.

Nagarjuna (1st-2nd centuries A.D.)

༄༅། །བཤེས་པའི་སྤྲིང་ཡིག་ཅེས་བྱ་བ་བཞུགས་སོ། །

རྒྱ་གར་སྐད་དུ། སུ་ཧྲི་ད་ལེ་ཁ།
བོད་སྐད་དུ། བཤེས་པའི་སྤྲིང་ཡིག །

འཇམ་དཔལ་གཞོན་ནུར་གྱུར་པ་ལ་ཕྱག་འཚལ་ལོ། །

ཡོན་ཏན་རང་བཞིན་དགེ་འོས་བདག་གིས་ནི། །
བདེ་བར་གཤེགས་པའི་གསུང་བསྙད་ལས་བྱུང་བའི། །
བསོད་ནམས་འདུན་སླད་འཕགས་པའི་དབྱངས་འདི་དག །
ཅུང་ཟད་ཅིག་བསྒྲིབས་ཁྱོད་ཀྱིས་གསན་པར་རིགས། །

ཇི་ལྟར་བདེ་གཤེགས་སྐུ་གཟུགས་ཤིང་ལས་ཀྱང་། །
བགྲིས་པ་ཅི་འདྲའང་རུང་སྟེ་མཁས་པས་མཆོད། །
དེ་བཞིན་བདག་གི་སྙན་ངག་འདི་ངན་ཡང་། །
དམ་ཆོས་བརྗོད་ལ་བསྟེན་སླད་སྨད་མི་བགྱིད། །

ཐུབ་པ་ཆེན་པོའི་བཀའ་འདི་སྙན་དགུ་ཞིག། །
ཁྱོད་ཀྱི་ཐུགས་སུ་ལྷ་ཡང་རྒྱུད་མོད་ཀྱི། །
རྗེ་ཐལ་ལས་བགྲིས་དཀར་ཟླའི་འོད་ཀྱིས་ནི། །
ཆེས་དཀར་ཉིད་དུ་ཅི་སྟེ་མི་བགྱིད་ལགས། །

Nagarjuna's *Letter to a Friend*

In Sanskrit: Suhrillekha
In Tibetan: bshes pa'i spring yig
In English: Letter to a Friend

Homage to the Gentle and Glorious Youth (Mañjugosha).

1
Listen now to these few lines of noble song
That I've composed for those with many virtues, fit for good,
To help them yearn for merit springing from
The sacred words of He Who's Gone to Bliss.

2
The wise will always honor and bow down
To Buddha statues, though they're made of wood;
So too, although these lines of mine be poor,
Do not feel scorn, they teach the Holy Way.

3
While you have surely learned and understood
The Mighty Buddha's many lovely words,
Is it not so that something made of chalk
By moonlight lit shines gleaming whiter still?

རྒྱལ་བས་སངས་རྒྱས་ཆོས་དང་དགེ་འདུན་དང་། །
གཏོང་དང་ཚུལ་ཁྲིམས་ལྷ་རྗེས་དྲན་པ་དྲུག །
རབ་ཏུ་བཀའ་སྩལ་དེ་དག་སོ་སོ་ཡི། །
ཡོན་ཏན་ཚོགས་ཀྱི་རྗེས་སུ་དྲན་པར་བགྱིད། །

དགེ་བའི་ལས་ལམ་བཅུ་པོ་ལུས་དང་ནི། །
ངག་དང་ཡིད་ཀྱིས་རྟག་ཏུ་བསྟེན་བགྱིད་ཅིང་། །
ཆང་རྣམས་ལས་ལྡོག་དེ་བཞིན་དགེ་བ་ཡི། །
འཚོ་བ་ལ་ཡང་མངོན་པར་དགྱེས་པར་མཛོད། །

ལོངས་སྤྱོད་གཡོ་བ་སྙིང་པོ་མེད་མཁྱེན་ནས། །
དགེ་སློང་བྲམ་ཟེ་བཀྲེན་དང་བཤེས་རྣམས་ལ། །
སྦྱིན་པ་ཚུལ་བཞིན་སྩོལ་བགྱི་ཕ་རོལ་ཏུ། །
སྦྱིན་ལས་གཞན་པའི་གཉེན་མཆོག་མ་མཆིས་སོ། །

ཁྱོད་ཀྱིས་ཚུལ་ཁྲིམས་མ་ཉམས་མོད་མི་དམའ། །
མ་འདྲེས་མ་སྦགས་པ་དག་བསྟེན་པར་མཛོད། །
ཁྲིམས་ནི་རྒྱུ་དང་མི་རྒྱུའི་ས་བཞིན་དུ། །
ཡོན་ཏན་ཀུན་གྱི་གཞི་རྟེན་ལགས་པར་གསུངས། །

སྦྱིན་དང་ཚུལ་ཁྲིམས་བཟོད་བརྩོན་བསམ་གཏན་དང་། །
དེ་བཞིན་ཤེས་རབ་གཞལ་མེད་ཕ་རོལ་ཕྱིན། །
འདི་དག་རྒྱས་མཛོད་སྲིད་པའི་རྒྱ་མཚོ་ཡི། །
ཕ་རོལ་ཕྱིན་པ་རྒྱལ་བའི་དབང་པོར་མཛོད། །

4
Six things there are the Buddhas have explained,
And all their virtues you must keep in mind:
The Buddha, Dharma, Sangha, bounteous acts,
And moral laws and gods—each one recall.

5
With body, speech, and mind always rely
On wholesome deeds, the tenfold virtuous path.
Avoiding liquor at all costs, thus find
True joy to lead a life of virtuous deeds.

6
Possessions are ephemeral and essenceless—
Know this and give them generously to monks,
To brahmins, to the poor, and to your friends:
Beyond there is no greater friend than gift.

7
Keep your vows unbroken, undegraded,
Uncorrupted, and quite free of stain.
Just as the earth's the base for all that's still or moves,
On discipline, it's said, is founded all that's good.

8
Generosity and discipline, patience, diligence,
Concentration, and the wisdom that knows thusness—
Those measureless perfections, make them grow,
And be a Mighty Conqueror who's crossed samsara's sea.

གང་ལ་ཕ་དང་མ་དག་མཆོད་བྱེད་པའི། །
རིགས་དེ་ཚངས་བཅས་སློབ་དཔོན་བཅས་པ་འདང་ལགས། །
དེ་དག་ལ་མཆོད་གྲགས་པར་འགྱུར་བ་དང་། །
སླད་མ་ལ་ཡང་མཐོ་རིས་ཐོབ་འགྱུར་ལགས། །

འཚེ་དང་ཆོམ་རྐུན་འཁྲིག་པ་བརྫུན་དང་ནི། །
ཆང་དང་དུས་མིན་ཟས་ལ་ཆགས་པ་དང་། །
མལ་སྟན་མཐོ་ལ་དགའ་དང་གླུ་དག་དང་། །
གར་དང་ཕྲེང་བའི་ཁྱད་པར་རྣམས་སྤོང་ཞིང་། །

དགྲ་བཅོམ་ཚུལ་ཁྲིམས་རྗེས་སུ་བྱེད་པ་ཡི། །
ཡན་ལག་བརྒྱད་པོ་འདི་དག་དང་ལྡན་ན། །
གསོ་སྦྱོང་འདོད་སྤྱོད་ལྷ་ལུས་ཡིད་འོང་བ། །
སྐྱེས་པ་བུད་མེད་དག་ལ་སྩོལ་བར་བགྱིད། །

སེར་སྣ་གཡོ་སྒྱུ་ཆགས་དང་སློམ་ལས་དང་། །
མངོན་པའི་ང་རྒྱལ་འདོད་ཆགས་ཞེ་སྡང་དང་། །
རིགས་དང་གཟུགས་དང་ཐོས་པ་ལང་ཚོ་དང་། །
དབང་ཐང་ཆེ་བའི་རྒྱགས་དགེ་དགྲ་བཞིན་གཟིགས། །

བག་ཡོད་བདུད་རྩིའི་གནས་ཏེ་བག་མེད་པ། །
འཆི་བའི་གནས་སུ་ཐུབ་པས་བཀའ་སྩལ་ཏེ། །
དེ་བས་ཁྱོད་ཀྱི་དགེ་ཆོས་སྤེལ་སླད་དུ། །
གུས་པས་རྟག་ཏུ་བག་དང་བཅས་པར་མཛོད། །

9
Those who show their parents great respect
With Brahma or a Master will be linked;
By venerating them they'll win repute,
In future they'll attain the higher realms.

10
Eschew all harm, don't steal, make love, or lie,
Abstain from drink, untimely greed for food,
Indulging in high beds, and singing too,
Refrain from dancing, all adornments shun.

11
For men and women who keep this eight-branched vow
And emulate the vows the Arhats took,
Their wish to nurture and to cleanse will grant
Them handsome bodies as celestial gods.

12
Stinginess and cunning, greed and sloth
And arrogance, attachment, hate, and pride
("I've breeding, good looks, learning, youth, and power")—
Such traits are seen as enemies of good.

13
Carefulness is the way to deathlessness,
While carelessness is death, the Buddha taught.
And thus, so that your virtuous deeds may grow,
Be careful, constantly and with respect.

གང་ཞིག་སྔོན་ཆད་བག་མེད་གྱུར་པ་ལ། །
ཕྱིནས་བག་དང་ལྡན་པར་གྱུར་དེ་ཡང་། །
ཟླ་བ་སྤྲིན་བྲལ་བཞིན་དུ་རྣམ་མཛེས་ཏེ། །
དགའ་བོ་སོར་ཕྲེང་མཐོང་ལྡན་བདེ་བྱེད་བཞིན། །

འདི་ལྟར་བཟོད་མཚུངས་དཀའ་ཐུབ་མ་མཆིས་པས། །
ཁྱོད་ཀྱིས་ཁྲོ་བའི་གོ་སྐབས་དབྱེ་མི་བགྱི། །
ཁྲོ་བ་སྤངས་པས་ཕྱིར་མི་ལྡོག་པ་ཉིད། །
འཐོབ་པར་འགྱུར་བ་སངས་རྒྱས་ཞལ་གྱིས་བཞེས། །

བདག་ནི་འདིས་སྤྱོས་འདིས་བཏག་ཕམ་པར་བྱས། །
འདི་ཡིས་བདག་གི་ནོར་འཕྲོག་གྱུར་ཏོ་ཞེས། །
ཁོན་དུ་འཛིན་པས་འཁྲུག་ལོང་རྣམས་སྐྱེད་དེ། །
ཁོན་འཛིན་རྣམ་སྤངས་བདེ་བར་གཉིད་ལོག་འགྱུར། །

སེམས་ནི་ཆུ་དང་ས་དང་རྡོ་བ་ལ། །
རི་མོར་བྲིས་པ་དེ་འདྲར་རིག་པར་བགྱི། །
དེའི་ནང་ཉོན་མོངས་ཅན་ལ་དང་པོ་ནི། །
མཆོག་སྟེ་ཆོས་འདོད་རྣམས་ལ་ཐམ་ལགས། །

རྒྱལ་བས་སྙིང་ལ་འབབ་དང་བདེན་པ་དང་། །
ལོག་པར་སྨྲ་ལྡན་སྐྱེས་བུ་རྣམས་ཀྱི་ནི། །
སྦྲང་རྩི་མེ་ཏོག་མི་གཙང་ལྟ་བུའི་ཚིག །
རྣམ་གསུམ་བཀའ་སྩལ་དེ་ལས་ཐམ་སྤང་། །

14
Those who formerly were careless
But then took heed are beautiful and fair,
As is the moon emerging from the clouds,
Like Nanda, Angulimala, Darshaka, Udayana.

15
Hard to practice, patience knows no peer,
So never allow yourself a moment's rage.
Avoid all anger and you will become
A Non-Returner, so the Buddha said.

16
"He's abused me, struck, defeated me,
And all my money too he has purloined!"
To harbor such resentment leads to strife;
Give up your grudge and sleep will easily come.

17
Understand your thoughts to be like figures drawn
On water, sandy soil, or carved in stone.
Of these, for tainted thoughts the first's the best,
While when you long for Dharma, it's the last.

18
Three kinds of speech are used by humankind,
And these the Victor variously described:
Like honey, sweet; like flowers, true; like filth,
Improper speech—the last of these eschew.

སྣང་ནས་སྣང་བའི་མཐར་ཐུག་མུན་པ་ནས། །
མུན་པའི་མཐར་ཐུག་སྣང་ནས་མུན་མཐར་ཐུག །
མུན་ནས་སྣང་བའི་མཐར་ཐུག་གང་ཟག་ནི། །
བཞི་སྟེ་དེ་དག་རྣམས་ཀྱི་དང་པོར་མཛོད། །

མི་ནི་ཨ་མྲའི་འབྲས་བཞིན་མ་སྨིན་ལ། །
སྨིན་པ་དང་འདྲ་སྨིན་ལ་མ་སྨིན་འདྲ། །
མ་སྨིན་མ་སྨིན་པར་ཡང་སྨིན་པ་ལ། །
སྨིན་པར་སྣང་ཞེས་བགྱི་བ་འདྲར་རྟོགས་མཛོད། །

གཞན་གྱི་ཆུང་མ་མི་བལྟ་མཐོང་ན་ཡང་། །
ན་ཚོད་མཐུན་པར་མ་དང་བུ་མོ་དང་། །
སྲིང་མོའི་འདུ་ཤེས་བསྐྱེད་བགྱི་ཆགས་གྱུར་ན། །
མི་གཙང་ཉིད་དུ་ཡང་དག་བསམ་པར་བགྱི། །

གཡོ་བའི་སེམས་ནི་ཐོས་མཚུངས་བུ་ལྟ་བུར། །
གཏེར་བཞིན་སྲོག་དང་འདྲ་བར་བསྲུང་བགྱི་སྟེ། །
གདུག་པ་དུག་དང་མཚོན་དང་དགྲ་བོ་དང་། །
མེ་བཞིན་འདོད་པའི་བདེ་ལ་ཡིད་འབྱུང་མཛོད། །

འདོད་པ་རྣམས་ནི་ཕུང་ཁྲོལ་སྐྱེད་པ་སྟེ། །
རྒྱལ་བའི་དབང་པོས་ཀིམ་པའི་འབྲས་འདྲར་གསུངས། །
དེ་དག་སྤང་བགྱི་དེ་ཡི་ལྕགས་སྒྲོག་གིས། །
འཁོར་བའི་བཙོན་རར་འཇིག་རྟེན་འདི་དག་བཅིངས། །

19
Some there are who go from light to light,
And some whose end from dark is darkness still,
While some from light to dark, or dark to light
End up, thus four, of these be as the first.

20
Men, like mangoes, can be sour and yet look ripe,
Some though ripe look green, and others green
Are sour indeed, while others still look ripe
And ripe they are: from this know how to act.

21
Do not gaze on others' wives, but if you do,
Regard them as your mother, child, or sib,
Depending on their age. Should lust arise,
Think well: they are by nature unclean filth.

22
Guard this fickle mind as you would do
Your learning, children, treasure, or your life.
Renounce all sensual pleasure as if it were
A viper, poison, weapon, foe, or fire.

23
The pleasures we desire will bring us ruin,
They're like the kimba fruit, the Buddha said.
Eschew them, it's their chains that tightly bind
The worldly in samsara's prison-house.

གང་དག་དབང་པོ་དྲུག་ཡུལ་རྣམས་ལ་ནི། །
རྟག་ཏུ་མི་བརྟན་གཡོ་དང་གང་དག་གཅིག །
གཡུལ་ངོར་དགྲ་ཚོགས་ལས་རྒྱལ་དེ་དག་ལས། །
མཁས་རྣམས་དང་པོ་དཔའ་རབ་ལགས་པར་འཚལ། །

བུད་མེད་གཞོན་ནུའི་ལུས་ནི་ལོགས་ཤིག་ཏུ། །
དྲི་ང་བ་དང་སྐྱོ་དགུ་རྡོད་པ་དང་། །
མི་གཙང་ཀུན་སྣོད་འདྲ་བ་དགང་དཀའ་དང་། །
པགས་པས་གཡོགས་དང་རྒྱན་ཡང་ལོགས་ཤིག་གཟིགས། །

ཇི་ལྟར་མཛེ་ཅན་སྲིན་བུས་ཉེན་པ་ནི། །
བདེ་བ་དོན་དུ་མེ་ལ་ཀུན་བསྟེན་ཀྱང་། །
ཞི་བར་མི་འགྱུར་དེ་དང་འདྲ་བར་ནི། །
འདོད་པ་རྣམས་ལ་ཆགས་པའང་མཁྱེན་པར་མཛོད། །

དོན་དམ་གཟིགས་པར་བགྱི་སླད་དངོས་རྣམས་ལ། །
ཚུལ་བཞིན་ཡིད་ལ་བགྱིད་པ་དེ་གོམས་མཛོད། །
དེ་དང་འདྲ་བའི་ཡོན་ཏན་ལྡན་པ་ཡི། །
ཆོས་གཞན་འགའ་ཡང་མཆིས་པ་མ་ལགས་སོ། །

སྐྱེས་བུ་རིགས་གཟུགས་ཐོས་དང་ལྡན་རྣམས་ཀྱང་། །
ཤེས་རབ་ཚུལ་ཁྲིམས་བྲལ་བ་བཀུར་མ་ལགས། །
དེ་ལྟས་གང་ལ་ཡོན་ཏན་འདི་གཉིས་ལྡན། །
དེ་ནི་ཡོན་ཏན་གཞན་དང་བྲལ་ཡང་མཆོད། །

24
Of he whose fickle senses are controlled—
These six that never cease to dart at things—
And he who's fought and conquered many foes,
The first is truly brave, the wise have said.

25
Regard a young girl's body on its own,
Its smell so foul, its openings nine—a pot
Of filth, insatiable, and clothed with skin.
Regard too her adornments on their own.

26
A man with leprosy, consumed by germs,
Will stand before the fire for comfort's sake
But still find no relief, so know the same is true
For those attached to the pleasures they desire.

27
In order that you see the absolute,
Get used to truly understanding things.
No other practice is there such as this
Possessed of special virtues such as these.

28
To those possessed of breeding, learning, handsome looks,
Who have no wisdom, neither discipline, you need not bow.
But those who do have these two qualities,
Though lacking other virtues, you should revere.

འཇིག་རྟེན་མཁྱེན་པ་རྙེད་དང་མ་རྙེད་དང་། །
བདེ་དང་མི་བདེ་སྙན་དང་མི་སྙན་དང་། །
བསྟོད་སྨད་ཅེས་བགྱི་འཇིག་རྟེན་ཆོས་བརྒྱད་པོ། །
བདག་གི་ཡིད་ཡུལ་མིན་པར་མགོ་སྙོམས་མཛོད། །

ཁྱོད་ཀྱིས་བྲམ་ཟེ་དགེ་སློང་ལྷ་དང་ནི། །
མགྲོན་དང་ཡབ་ཡུམ་དག་དང་བཙུན་མོ་དང་། །
འཁོར་གྱི་སླད་དུའང་སྡིག་པ་མི་བགྱི་སྟེ། །
དམྱལ་བའི་རྣམ་སྨིན་སྐལ་ནོད་འགའ་མ་མཆིས། །

སྡིག་པའི་ལས་རྣམས་བྱེད་པ་འགའ་ཡང་ནི། །
དེ་ཡི་མོད་ལ་མཚོན་བཞིན་མི་གཅོད་ཀྱང་། །
འཆི་བའི་དུས་ལ་བབ་ན་སྡིག་པ་ཡི། །
ལས་ཀྱི་འབྲས་བུ་གང་ལགས་མངོན་པར་འགྱུར། །

དད་དང་ཚུལ་ཁྲིམས་ཐོས་དང་གཏོང་བ་དང་། །
དྲི་མེད་ངོ་ཚ་ཤེས་དང་ཁྲེལ་ཡོད་དང་། །
ཤེས་རབ་ནོར་བདུན་ལགས་པར་ཐུབ་པས་གསུངས། །
ནོར་གཞན་ཕལ་པ་དོན་མ་མཆིས་རྟོགས་མཛོད། །

རྒྱན་པོ་འགྱེད་དང་འདུས་ལ་ལྟ་བ་དང་། །
ལེ་ལོ་སྡིག་པའི་གྲོགས་ལ་བརྟེན་པ་དང་། །
ཆང་དང་མཚན་མོ་རྒྱུ་བ་ངན་སོང་དུ། །
གྲགས་པ་ཉམས་པར་འགྱུར་བའི་དེ་དྲུག་སྤོངས། །

29
You who know the world, take gain and loss,
Or bliss and pain, or kind words and abuse,
Or praise and blame—these eight mundane concerns—
Make them the same, and don't disturb your mind.

30
Perform no evil, even for the sake
Of brahmins, bhikshus, gods, or honored guests,
Your father, mother, queen, or for your court.
The ripened fruit in hell's for you alone.

31
Although performing wrong and evil deeds
Does not at once, like swords, create a gash,
When death arrives, those evil acts will show,
Their karmic fruit will clearly be revealed.

32
Faith and ethics, learning, bounteousness,
A flawless sense of shame and decency,
And wisdom are the seven riches Buddha taught.
Know, other common riches have no worth.

33
Gambling, public spectacles and shows,
And indolence, bad company, strong drink,
And nightly prowls—these six will lead to lower realms
And damage your good name, so give them up.

ནོར་རྣམས་ཀུན་གྱི་ནང་ན་ཆོག་ཤེས་པ། །
རབ་མཆོག་ལགས་པར་ལྷ་མིའི་སྟོན་པས་གསུངས། །
ཀུན་ཏུ་ཆོག་ཤེས་མཛོད་ཅིག་ཆོག་མཁྱེན་ན། །
ནོར་མི་བདོག་ཀྱང་ཡང་དག་འབྱོར་བ་ལགས། །

དེས་པ་བདོག་མང་ཇི་ལྟར་སྡུག་བསྔལ་བ། །
འདོད་པ་ཆུང་རྣམས་དེ་ལྟ་མ་ལགས་ཏེ། །
ཀླུ་མཆོག་རྣམས་ལ་མགོ་བོ་ཇི་སྙེད་པ། །
དེ་ལས་བྱུང་བའི་སྡུག་བསྔལ་དེ་སྙེད་དོ། །

རང་བཞིན་དགྲ་འབྲེལ་གཤེད་མ་ལྟ་བུ་དང་། །
ཁྱིམ་ཐབས་བརྙས་བགྱི་ཇོ་མོ་ལྟ་བུ་དང་། །
ཆུང་དུའང་རྐུ་བ་ཆོམ་རྐུན་ལྟ་བུ་ཡི། །
ཆུང་མ་གསུམ་པོ་དེ་ཡང་རྣམ་པར་སྤང་། །

སྲིང་མོ་ལྟ་བུར་རྗེས་མཐུན་གང་ཡིན་དང་། །
མཛའ་མོ་བཞིན་དུ་སྙིང་ལ་འབབ་པ་དང་། །
མ་བཞིན་ཕན་པར་འདོད་དང་བྲན་མོ་བཞིན། །
དབང་གྱུར་གང་ཡིན་རིགས་ཀྱི་ལྷ་བཞིན་བཀུར། །

ཁ་ཟས་སྨན་དང་འདྲ་བར་རིགས་པ་ཡིས། །
འདོད་ཆགས་ཞེ་སྡང་མེད་པར་བསྟེན་བགྱི་སྟེ། །
རྒྱགས་ཕྱིར་མ་ལགས་བསྙེམས་པའི་ཕྱིར་མ་ལགས། །
མཚག་ཕྱིར་མ་ལགས་ལུས་གནས་འབའ་ཞིག་ཕྱིར། །

34
Of all great wealth, contentment is supreme,
Said he who taught and guided gods and men.
So always be content; if you know this
Yet have no wealth, true riches you'll have found.

35
Kind Sir, to own a lot brings so much misery,
There's no such grief for those with few desires.
The more the naga lords possess of heads,
The more their headaches, the more they have of cares.

36
A murderess who sides with enemies,
A queen who holds her husband in contempt,
A thieving wife who steals the smallest thing—
It's these three kinds of wife you must avoid.

37
A wife who like a sister follows you,
Affectionate like a true and loving friend,
Supportive like a mother, obedient like a maid—
She must be honored like a family god.

38
Take food as medicine, in the right amount,
Without attachment, without hatefulness:
Don't eat for vanity, for pride or ego's sake,
Eat only for your body's sustenance.

རིགས་པའི་བདག་ཉིད་ཉིན་པར་མཐའ་དག་དང་། །
མཚན་མོ་ཐུན་གྱི་སྟོད་སྨད་བཟླས་ནས་ནི། །
མནལ་ཆོའང་འབྲས་བུ་མེད་པར་མི་འགྱུར་བར། །
དྲན་དང་ལྡན་པར་དེ་དག་བར་དུ་མནོལ། །

བྱམས་དང་སྙིང་རྗེ་དག་དང་དགའ་བ་དང་། །
བཏང་སྙོམས་རྟག་ཏུ་ཡང་དག་སྒོམ་མཛོད་ཅིག །
གོང་མ་བརྙེས་པར་མ་གྱུར་དེ་ལྟ་ནའང་། །
ཚངས་པའི་འཇིག་རྟེན་བདེ་བ་ཐོབ་པར་འགྱུར། །

འདོད་སྤྱོད་དགའ་དང་བདེ་དང་སྡུག་བསྔལ་དག །
རྣམ་པར་སྤངས་པའི་བསམ་གཏན་བཞི་པོ་ཡིས། །
ཚངས་རིས་འོད་གསལ་དག་དང་དགེ་རྒྱས་དང་། །
འབྲས་བུ་ཆེ་ལྷ་རྣམས་དང་སྐལ་མཉམ་འཐོབ། །

རྟག་དང་མངོན་པར་ཞེན་དང་གཉེན་པོ་མེད། །
ཡོན་ཏན་གཙོ་ལྡན་གཞི་ལས་བྱུང་བའི་ལས། །
དགེ་དང་མི་དགེ་རྣམ་ལྔ་ཆེན་པོ་སྟེ། །
དེ་བས་དགེ་བ་སྤྱོད་ལ་བརྩོན་པར་བགྱི། །

ལན་ཚྭ་སྲང་འགས་ཆུ་ནི་ཉུང་ངུ་ཞིག །
རོ་བསྒྱུར་ནུས་ཀྱི་གངྒཱི་ཀླུང་མིན་ལྟར། །
དེ་བཞིན་སྡིག་པའི་ལས་ནི་ཆུང་ངུ་ཡང་། །
དགེ་བའི་རྩ་བ་ཡངས་ལ་མཁྱེན་པར་བགྱི། །

39
O Knowledgeable One, recite all day
And in the first and last watch of the night.
Then in between these two sleep mindfully
So that your slumbers are not spent in vain.

40
Constantly and perfectly reflect
On love, compassion, joy, impartiality.
And should you not attain the higher state,
At least you will find bliss in Brahma's world.

41
The four samadhis, which in turn discard
Pursuit of pleasure, joy and bliss and pain,
Will lead to fortune equal to the gods'
In Brahma, Light, Great Virtue, or Great Fruit.

42
Great good and evil deeds are of five kinds,
Determined by their constancy, their zeal,
Their lack of counteragent, their perfect fields.
So strive in this respect to practice good.[1]

43
A pinch of salt can give its salty taste
To a little water, but not to the Ganges stream.
So know that, likewise, minor evil deeds
Can never change a mighty source of good.

རྒོད་དང་འགྱོད་དང་མནོད་སེམས་རྨུགས་པ་དང་། །
གཉིད་དང་འདོད་ལ་འདུན་དང་ཐེ་ཚོམ་སྟེ། །
སྒྲིབ་པ་ལྔ་པོ་འདི་དག་དགེ་བའི་ནོར། །
འཕྲོག་པའི་ཆོམ་རྐུན་ལགས་པར་མཁྱེན་པར་མཛོད། །

དད་དང་བརྩོན་འགྲུས་དག་དང་དྲན་པ་དང་། །
ཏིང་འཛིན་ཤེས་རབ་ཆོས་མཆོག་ལྔ་ཉིད་དེ། །
འདི་ལ་མངོན་བརྩོན་མཛོད་ཅིག་འདི་དག་ནི། །
སྟོབས་དབང་ཞེས་བགྱི་རྩེ་མོར་གྱུར་པའང་ལགས། །

ན་རྒ་འཆི་སྡུག་བྲལ་དང་དེ་བཞིན་དུ། །
ལས་ནི་བདག་གི་བྱས་ལས་མ་འདས་ཞེས། །
དེ་ལྟར་ཡང་དང་ཡང་དུ་སེམས་པ་ནི། །
དེ་ཡི་གཉེན་པོའི་སྙོམས་རྒྱགས་མི་འགྱུར། །

གལ་ཏེ་མཐོ་རིས་ཐར་པ་མངོན་བཞེད་ན། །
ཡང་དག་ལྟ་ལ་གོམས་པ་ཉིད་དུ་མཛོད། །
གང་ཟག་ལོག་པར་ལྟ་བས་ལེགས་སྤྱད་ཀྱང་། །
ཐམས་ཅད་རྣམ་པར་སྨིན་པ་མི་བཟད་ལྡན། །

མི་ནི་ཡང་དག་ཉིད་དུ་མི་བདེ་ཞིང་། །
མི་རྟག་བདག་མེད་མི་གཙང་རིག་པར་བགྱི། །
དྲན་པ་ཉེ་བར་མ་གཞག་རྣམས་ཀྱིས་ནི། །
ཕྱིན་ཅི་ལོག་བཞིར་ལྟ་བ་ཕུང་བྲོལ་བ། །

44
Wildness and remorse, and hateful thoughts,
And dullness-somnolence, and yearning lust,
And doubt are hindrances—please know these five
Are thieves that steal the gem of virtuous deeds.

45
With faith and diligence and mindfulness,
And concentration, wisdom, five in all,
You must strive hard to reach the "highest state":
As "powers" these "forces" take you to the "peak."

46
"I'm not beyond my karma, the deeds I've done;
I'll still fall ill, age, die, and leave my friends."
Think like this again and yet again
And with this remedy avoid all arrogance.

47
If higher birth and freedom is your quest,
You must become accustomed to right views.
Those who practice good with inverse views
Will yet experience terrible results.

48
Know this truth: that men are ever sad,
Impermanent, devoid of self, impure.
Those who do not have close mindfulness,
Their view four times inverted, head for ruin.

གཟུགས་ནི་བདག་མ་ཡིན་ཞེས་གསུངས་ཏེ་བདག །
གཟུགས་དང་ལྡན་མིན་གཟུགས་ལ་བདག་གནས་མིན། །
བདག་ལ་གཟུགས་མི་གནས་ཏེ་དེ་བཞིན་དུ། །
ཕུང་པོ་ལྷག་མ་བཞི་ཡང་སྟོང་རྟོགས་བགྱི། །

ཕུང་པོ་འདོད་རྒྱལ་ལས་མིན་དུས་ལས་མིན། །
རང་བཞིན་ལས་མིན་ངོ་བོ་ཉིད་ལས་མིན། །
དབང་ཕྱུག་ལས་མིན་རྒྱུ་མེད་ཅན་མིན་ཏེ། །
མི་ཤེས་ལས་དང་སྲེད་ལས་བྱུང་རིག་མཛོད། །

ཚུལ་ཁྲིམས་བརྟུལ་ཞུགས་མཆོག་འཛིན་རང་ལུས་ལ། །
ཕྱིན་ཅི་ལོག་པར་ལྟ་དང་ཐེ་ཚོམ་སྟེ། །
ཀུན་ཏུ་སྦྱོར་བ་འདི་གསུམ་ཐར་པ་ཡི། །
གྲོང་ཁྱེར་སྒོ་འགེགས་ལགས་པར་མཁྱེན་པར་གྱིས། །

ཐར་པ་བདག་ལ་རག་ལས་འདི་ལ་ནི། །
གཞན་གྱིས་གྲོགས་བགྱིར་ཅི་ཡང་མ་མཆིས་པས། །
ཐོས་དང་ཚུལ་ཁྲིམས་བསམ་གཏན་ལྡན་པ་ཡིས། །
བདེན་པ་རྣམ་པ་བཞི་ལ་འབད་པ་མཛོད། །

ལྷག་པའི་ཚུལ་ཁྲིམས་ལྷག་པའི་ཤེས་རབ་དང་། །
ལྷག་པའི་སེམས་ལ་རྟག་ཏུ་བསླབ་པར་བགྱི། །
བསླབ་པ་བརྒྱ་རྩ་ལྔ་བཅུ་ལྷག་གཅིག་སྟེ། །
གསུམ་པོ་འདི་ནང་ཡང་དག་འདུ་བར་འགྱུར། །

49
Form is not the self, the Buddha taught,
And self does not have form, nor dwell in form,
While form dwells not in self. Thus you must see
The four remaining aggregates are empty too.

50
The aggregates are not a simple whim,
From neither time nor nature do they come,
Nor by themselves, from God, or without cause;
Their source, you ought to know, is ignorance,
From karmic deeds and craving have they come.

51
To feel that one is ethically superior,
To view one's body wrongly, and to doubt—
With these three fetters, you should understand,
The way through freedom's city gates is blocked.

52
Freedom will depend on you alone
And there is no one else, no friend can help.
So bring endeavor to the Four Noble Truths
With study, discipline, and concentration.

53
Train always in superior discipline,
Superior wisdom, and superior mind.
Monks' vows exceed a hundred and five tens,
Yet they are all included in these three.

དབང་ཕྱུག་ལུས་གཏོགས་དྲན་པ་བདེ་གཤེགས་ཀྱིས། །
བགྲོད་པ་གཅིག་པའི་ལམ་དུ་ཉེ་བར་བསྟན། །
དེ་ནི་བསྒྲིམས་ནས་མངོན་པར་བསྲུང་བགྱི་སྟེ། །
དྲན་པ་ཉམས་པས་ཆོས་ཀུན་འཇིག་པར་འགྱུར། །

ཚེ་ནི་གནོད་མང་རླུང་གིས་བཏབ་པ་ཡི། །
ཆུ་ཡི་ཆུ་བུར་བས་ཀྱང་མི་རྟག་ན། །
དབུགས་རྔུབ་དབུགས་འབྱུང་གཉིད་ཀྱི་ཡོག་པ་ལས། །
སད་ཁོམ་གང་ལགས་དེ་ནི་ངོ་མཚར་ཆེ། །

ལུས་མཐའ་ཐལ་བ་མཐར་སྐམ་མཐར་འདྲུལ་ཞིང་། །
ཐ་མར་མི་གཙང་སྙིང་པོ་མ་མཆིས་པ། །
རྣམ་པར་འཇིག་དེངས་སྨྱུགས་པར་འགྱུར་བ་སྟེ། །
སོ་སོར་འགྲེས་ཆོས་ཅན་དུ་མཁྱེན་པར་མཛོད། །

ས་དང་ལྷུན་པོ་རྒྱ་མཚོ་ཉི་མ་བདུན། །
འབར་བས་བསྲེགས་པའི་ལུས་ཅན་འདི་དག་ཀྱང་། །
ཐལ་བ་ཙམ་ཡང་ལུས་པར་མི་འགྱུར་ན། །
ཤིན་ཏུ་ཉམས་ཆུང་མི་ལྟ་སྨོས་ཅི་འཚལ། །

དེ་ལྟར་འདི་ཀུན་མི་རྟག་བདག་མེད་དེ། །
སྐྱབས་མེད་མགོན་མེད་གནས་མེད་དེ་སླད་དུ། །
འཁོར་བ་ཆུ་ཤིང་སྙིང་པོ་མེད་པ་ལས། །
མི་མཆོག་ཁྱོད་ཀྱིས་ཐུགས་ནི་དབུགས་དབྱུང་མཛོད། །

54
My lord, the Buddha taught close mindfulness
Of body as the single path to tread.
Hold fast and guard it well, for all the Dharma
Is destroyed by loss of mindfulness.

55
With all its many risks, this life endures
No more than windblown bubbles in a stream.
How marvellous to breathe in and out again,
To fall asleep and then awake refreshed.

56
This body ends as ash, dry dust, or slime,
And ultimately shit, no essence left.
Consumed, evaporated, rotted down—
Thus know its nature: to disintegrate.

57
The ground, Mount Meru, and the oceans too
Will be consumed by seven blazing suns;
Of things with form no ashes will be left,
No need to speak of puny, frail man.

58
It's all impermanent, devoid of self,
So if you're not to stay there refugeless
And helpless, drag your mind away, O King,
From plantainlike samsara, which has no core.

རྒྱ་མཚོ་གཅིག་ནས་གཉའ་ཤིང་བུ་ག་དང་། །
རུས་སྦལ་ཕྲད་པ་བས་ཀྱང་དུད་འགྲོ་ལས། །
མི་ཉིད་ཆེས་ཐོབ་དཀའ་བས་མི་དབང་གིས། །
དམ་ཆོས་སྤྱོད་པས་དེ་འབྲས་མཆིས་པར་མཛོད། །

གང་ཞིག་གསེར་སྣོད་རིན་ཆེན་སྤྲས་པ་ཡིས། །
ངན་སྐྱུགས་འཕྱག་པར་བགྱིད་པ་དེ་བས་ཀྱང་། །
གང་ཞིག་མི་རུ་སྐྱེས་ནས་སྡིག་པ་དག །
བགྱིད་པ་དེ་ནི་ཆེས་རབ་བླུན་པ་ལགས། །

མཐུན་པར་གྱུར་པའི་ཡུལ་དུ་གནས་པ་དང་། །
སྐྱེས་བུ་དམ་པ་ལ་ནི་བསྟེན་པ་དང་། །
བདག་ཉིད་ལེགས་སྨོན་སྔོན་ཡང་བསོད་ནམས་བགྱིས། །
འཁོར་ལོ་ཆེན་པོ་བཞི་ནི་ཁྱོད་ལ་མངའ། །

དགེ་བའི་བཤེས་གཉེན་བསྟེན་པ་ཚངས་པར་སྤྱོད། །
ཡོངས་སུ་རྫོགས་པར་ཐུབ་པས་གསུངས་དེའི་ཕྱིར། །
སྐྱེས་བུ་དམ་པ་བསྟེན་བགྱི་རྒྱལ་བ་ལ། །
བརྟེན་ནས་རབ་ཏུ་མང་པོས་ཞི་བ་ཐོབ། །

ལོག་པར་ལྟ་བ་འཛིན་དང་དུད་འགྲོ་དང་། །
ཡི་དྭགས་ཉིད་དང་དམྱལ་བར་སྐྱེ་བ་དང་། །
རྒྱལ་བའི་བཀའ་མེད་པ་དང་མཐའ་འཁོབ་ཏུ། །
ཀླ་ཀློར་སྐྱེ་དང་གླེན་ཞིང་ལྐུགས་པ་ཉིད། །

59
Harder, harder still than that a turtle chance upon
The opening in a yoke upon a great and single sea
Is rebirth as a human after rebirth as a beast;
So heed the sacred Dharma, King, and make your life bear fruit.

60
More stupid yet than one who throws some slops
Into a golden vessel all bejewelled
Is he who's gained a precious human birth
And wastes it in an evil, sinful life.

61
To dwell in places that befit the task,
To follow and rely on holy beings,
Aspiring high, with merit from the past—
These four great wheels are yours for you to use.

62
The virtuous friend in whom to place your trust
Has brought pure conduct to perfection, said the Lord.
So follow holy beings, many are they
Who relied upon the Buddhas and found peace.

63
To be reborn with false beliefs, or yet
As animals, or pretas, or in hell,
Deprived of Buddha's words, barbarians
In border lands, or reborn dull and dumb,

ཚེ་རིང་ལྷ་ཉིད་གང་ཡང་རུང་བ་ནི། །
སྐྱེ་བ་ཞེས་བགྱི་མི་ཁོམ་སྐྱོན་བརྒྱད་པོ། །
དེ་དག་དང་བྲལ་ཁོམ་པ་རྙེད་ནས་ནི། །
སྐྱེ་བ་བཟློག་པའི་སླད་དུ་འབད་པར་མཛོད། །

དེས་པ་འདོད་པས་ཡོངས་དང་འཆི་བ་དང་། །
ན་དང་རྒ་སོགས་སྡུག་བསྔལ་དུ་མ་ཡི། །
འབྱུང་གནས་འཁོར་བ་ལ་ནི་སྐྱོ་མཛད་ཅིང་། །
འདི་ཡི་ཉེས་པའི་ཤས་ཀྱང་གསན་པར་མཛོད། །

ཕ་ནི་བུ་ཉིད་མ་ནི་ཆུང་མ་ཉིད། །
སྐྱེ་བོ་དགྲར་གྱུར་པ་དག་བཤེས་ཉིད་དང་། །
བཟློག་པ་ཉིད་དུ་མཆི་བས་དེ་སླད་དུ། །
འཁོར་བ་དག་ན་ངེས་པ་འགའ་མ་མཆིས། །

རེ་རེས་རྒྱ་མཚོ་བཞི་བས་ལྷག་པ་ཡི། །
འོ་མ་འཐུངས་ཏེ་ད་དུང་སོ་སོ་ཡི། །
སྐྱེ་བོའི་རྗེས་སུ་འབྲངས་བའི་འཁོར་བ་པས། །
དེ་བས་ཆེས་མང་ཉིད་ཅིག་བཏུང་འཚལ་ལོ། །

རེ་རེའི་བདག་ཉིད་རུས་པའི་ཕུང་པོ་ནི། །
ལྷུན་པོ་མཉམ་པ་སྙེད་ཅིག་འདས་གྱུར་ཏེ། །
མ་ཡི་ཐུག་མཐའ་རྒྱ་ཤུག་ཚིག་གུ་ཙམ། །
རི་ལ་བུར་བགྲངས་ཀྱང་ས་ཡིས་ལང་མི་འགྱུར། །

64
Or born among the long-lived gods—
Of these eight defective states that give no opportunity
You must be free, and, finding opportunity,
Be diligent, to put a stop to birth.

65
O Gentle Sir, to make your disenchantment grow
With this samsara, source of many pains—
Desires frustrated, death, ill health, old age—
Please heed its defects, even just a few.

66
Men who've fathered sons in turn are sons,
And mothers likewise daughters. Bitter foes
Turn into friends, the converse too is true.
Because of this samsara's never sure.

67
Know that every being has drunk more milk
Than all the four great oceans could contain,
And still, by emulating common folk,
They'll circle, drinking ever more and more.

68
A heap of all the bones each being has left
Would reach to Meru's top or even higher.
To count one's mother's lineage with pills
The size of berries, the earth would not suffice.

བརྒྱ་བྱིན་འཇིག་རྟེན་མཆོད་འོས་གྱུར་ནས་ནི། །
ལས་ཀྱི་དབང་གིས་ཕྱིར་ཡང་ས་སྟེང་ལྷུང་། །
འཁོར་ལོས་སྒྱུར་བ་ཉིད་དུ་གྱུར་ནས་ཀྱང་། །
འཁོར་བ་དག་ཏུ་ཡང་བྲན་ཉིད་དུ་འགྱུར། །

མཐོ་རིས་བུ་མོའི་ནུ་མ་སྐྱེད་པ་ལ། །
རེག་པའི་བདེ་བ་ཡུན་རིང་མྱོང་ནས་སླར། །
དམྱལ་བར་འཐག་གཅོད་དབད་པའི་འཁྲུལ་འཁོར་གྱི། །
རེག་པ་ཤིན་ཏུ་མི་བཟད་བསྟེན་འཚལ་ལོ། །

རྐང་པའི་རེག་པས་ནེམས་པར་བདེ་བཟོད་པ། །
ལྷུན་པོའི་སྤྱོ་ལ་ཡུན་རིང་གནས་ནས་ནི། །
སླར་ཡང་མེ་མུར་རོ་མྱགས་རྒྱུ་བ་ཡི། །
སྡུག་བསྔལ་མི་བཟད་ཡོག་སླམ་བགྱིད་འཚལ་ལོ། །

མཐོ་རིས་བུ་མོས་འཁྲོངས་ཤིང་དགའ་ཚལ་དང་། །
རྣམ་པར་མཛེས་ཚལ་སོན་པར་རྩེས་ནས་སླར། །
འདབ་མ་རལ་གྲི་འདྲ་ཚལ་ནགས་རྣམས་ཀྱིས། །
རྐང་ལག་རྣ་བ་སྣ་གཅོད་འཐོབ་པར་འགྱུར། །

དལ་གྱིས་འབབ་པ་ལྷ་ཡི་བུ་མོ་ནི། །
གདོང་མཛེས་གསེར་གྱི་པདྨ་ལྡན་ཞུགས་ནས། །
སླར་ཡང་དམྱལ་བའི་ཆུ་བོ་རབ་མེད་པར། །
ཚྭ་སྒོ་བཟོད་བརླག་ཆུ་ཆེན་འཇུག་འཚལ་ལོ། །

69
Indra, universally revered,
Will fall again to earth through action's force.
And he who ruled the universe as king
Will be a slave within samsara's wheel.

70
For ages it was rapture to caress
The lovely breasts and waists of heaven's maids,
Now one will bear the terrible caress—
The crush, the slash, and tear—of hell's machine.

71
For years you might have stayed on Meru's crest
Delighting as it yielded underfoot,
But think now of the torment that will strike:
To wade through glowing coals and rotten flesh.

72
Those who in the Joyous Garden played,
And in Beauty's Grove were served by heaven's maids,
Will come to woods of trees with swordlike leaves
And cut their hands and feet, their ears and nose.

73
Among the golden lotuses and lovely maids
They bathed in heaven's Gently Flowing Pool,
But into hell's own waters will they plunge,
The scalding, caustic River None Can Ford.

ལྷ་ཡུལ་འདོད་བདེ་ཤིན་ཏུ་ཆེན་པོ་དང་། །
ཚངས་ཉིད་ཆགས་བྲལ་བདེ་བ་ཐོབ་ནས་སླར། །
མནར་མེད་མེ་ཡི་བུད་ཤིང་གྱུར་པ་ཡི། །
སྡུག་བསྔལ་རྒྱུན་མི་འཆད་པ་བརྟེན་འཚལ་ལོ། །

ཉི་མ་ཟླ་བ་ཉིད་ཐོབ་རང་ལུས་ཀྱི། །
འོད་ཀྱིས་འཇིག་རྟེན་མཐའ་དག་སྣང་བྱས་ནས། །
སླར་ཡང་མུན་ནག་སྨག་ཏུ་ཕྱིན་གྱུར་ནས། །
རང་གི་ལག་པ་བརྐྱང་བའང་མི་མཐོང་འགྱུར། །

དེ་ལྟར་ནོངས་པར་འགྱུར་འཚལ་བསོད་ནམས་ནི། །
རྣམ་གསུམ་མར་མེའི་སྣང་བ་རབ་བཞེས་ཤིག །
གཅིག་པུར་ཉི་མ་ཟླ་བས་མི་བརྡི་བའི། །
མུན་ནག་མཐའ་དག་ནང་དུ་འཇུག་འཚལ་ལོ། །

སེམས་ཅན་ཉེས་པར་སྤྱོད་པ་སྤྱོད་རྣམས་ལ། །
ཡང་སོས་ཐིག་ནག་རབ་ཏུ་ཚ་བ་དང་། །
བསྡུས་འཇོམས་ངུ་འབོད་མནར་མེད་ལ་སོགས་པའི། །
དམྱལ་བ་རྣམས་སུ་རྟག་ཏུ་སྡུག་བསྔལ་འགྱུར། །

ཁ་ཅིག་ཏིལ་བཞིན་འཚིར་ཏེ་དེ་བཞིན་དུ། །
གཞན་ནི་ཕྱེ་མ་ཞིབ་བཞིན་ཕྱེ་མར་རློག །
ཁ་ཅིག་སོག་ལེས་འདྲ་སྟེ་དེ་བཞིན་གཞན། །
སྤུ་རི་མི་བཟད་སོ་རྣོན་རྣམས་ཀྱིས་གཤགས། །

74
A Kamaloka god, one gains such bliss,
As Brahma, bliss that's free from all desire;
But know that after that comes constant pain:
As firewood one feeds Avici's flames.

75
One who was reborn as sun or moon,
Whose body's light lit whole worlds far below,
Will then arrive in states of darkest gloom,
His outstretched hands will be invisible.

76
So thus it is you'll ail, and knowing this
Please seize the lamp of merit's triple form,
For otherwise you'll plunge and go alone
In deepest dark unlit by sun or moon.

77
For beings who indulge in evil deeds
There's constant pain in these and other hells:
Reviving Hell, Black Line, and Intense Heat,
And Crushing, Screaming, Torment Unsurpassed.

78
Some are squeezed and pressed like sesame,
Others likewise ground like finest flour,
Some are cut and carved as if with saws,
Others hacked with axes, razor-honed.

དེ་བཞིན་གཞན་དག་ཁྲོ་ཆུ་བཞུས་པ་ཡི། །
ཁུ་བ་འབར་བ་འབྲིགས་པ་ལྡུད་པར་བགྱིད། །
ཁ་ཅིག་ལྕགས་ཀྱི་གསལ་ལ་ཤིང་རབ་འབར་བ། །
ཚེར་མ་ཅན་ལ་ཀུན་ཏུ་རྒྱུད་པར་བགྱིད། །

ཁ་ཅིག་ལྕགས་ཀྱི་མཆེ་བ་ལྡན་པའི་ཁྱི། །
གཏུམ་པོས་དབད་ཅིང་ལག་པ་གནམ་དུ་བསྒྲེངས། །
དབང་མེད་གཞན་དག་ལྕགས་མཆུ་རྣོན་པོ་དང་། །
སེན་མོ་མི་བཟད་ལྡན་པའི་ཁྭ་རྣམས་འཐོག །

ཁ་ཅིག་སྲིན་བུ་སྦྲུར་པ་སྣ་ཚོགས་དང་། །
ཤ་སྦྲང་སྦྲང་མ་ནག་པོ་ཁྲི་ཕྲག་དག །
རེག་ན་མི་བཟད་རྨ་སྐྱོལ་ཆེར་འབྱིན་པས། །
ཟ་བར་བགྱིད་ཅིང་འགྲེ་ལྡོག་སྒྲེ་སྡུགས་འདོན། །

ཁ་ཅིག་མདག་མེ་འབར་བའི་ཚོགས་སུ་ནི། །
རྒྱུན་མི་འཆད་པར་རབ་བསྲེགས་ཁ་ཡང་བགྲད། །
ཁ་ཅིག་ལྕགས་ལས་བྱས་པའི་ཟངས་ཆེན་དུ། །
སྤྱི་འུ་ཚུགས་འབྲས་ཀྱི་ཐུང་འཕེང་བཞིན་དུ་འཚེད། །

སྡིག་ཅན་དབུགས་འབྱུང་འགགས་པ་ཙམ་ཞིག་གི། །
དུས་ཀྱིས་བར་དུ་ཚོད་རྣམས་དམྱལ་བ་ཡི། །
སྡུག་བསྔལ་གཞལ་ཡས་ཐོས་ནས་རྣམ་སྟོང་དུ། །
མི་འཇིགས་གང་ལགས་རྡོ་རྗེའི་རང་བཞིན་ནོ། །

79
Others still are forced to swallow draughts
Of burning molten bronze that flares and sparks,
Some impaled and threaded onto skewers—
Barbed and fiercely blazing stakes of steel.

80
Some, whom savage dogs with iron fangs
Will rip to shreds, in dread throw up their hands,
And others, powerless, are pecked by crows
With sharpened beaks of steel and razor claws.

81
Some there are who roll about and wail,
Devoured by worms and multicolored grubs,
Ten thousand buzzing flies and bees that leave
Great stings and bites unbearable to touch.

82
Some, in heaps of blazing red hot coals,
Are burned without a break, their mouths agape.
And some are boiled in cauldrons made of iron,
Cooked like dumplings, heads turned upside down.

83
The very instant that they cease to breathe
The wicked taste the boundless pains of hell.
And he who hearing this is not afraid
A thousandfold is truly diamond hard.

དམྱལ་བ་བྲིས་པ་མཐོང་དང་ཐོས་པ་དང་། །
དྲན་དང་བཀླགས་དང་གཟུགས་སུ་བགྱིས་རྣམས་ཀྱང་། །
འཇིགས་པ་སྐྱེད་པར་འགྱུར་ན་མི་བཟད་པའི། །
རྣམ་སྨིན་ཉམས་སུ་མྱོང་ན་སྨོས་ཅི་འཚལ། །

བདེ་བ་ཀུན་གྱི་ནང་ན་སྲེད་ཟད་པ། །
བདེ་བའི་བདག་པོར་བགྱིད་པ་ཇི་ལྟ་བར། །
དེ་བཞིན་སྡུག་བསྔལ་ཀུན་གྱི་ནང་ན་ནི། །
མནར་མེད་དམྱལ་བའི་སྡུག་བསྔལ་རབ་མི་བཟད། །

འདི་ན་ཉིན་གཅིག་མདུང་ཐུང་སུམ་བརྒྱ་ཡིས། །
རབ་ཏུ་དྲག་བཏབ་བསྡུག་བསྔལ་གང་ལགས་པ། །
དེས་ནི་དམྱལ་བའི་སྡུག་བསྔལ་ཆུང་ངུ་ལའང་། །
འོལ་ཡང་མི་བགྱི་ཆར་ཡང་མི་ཕོད་དོ། །

དེ་ལྟར་སྡུག་བསྔལ་ཤིན་ཏུ་མི་བཟད་ལོ། །
བྱེ་བ་ཕྲག་བརྒྱར་ཉམས་སུ་མྱོང་ཡང་ནི། །
ཇི་སྲིད་མི་དགེ་དེ་ཟད་མ་གྱུར་པ། །
དེ་སྲིད་སྲོག་དང་བྲལ་བར་མི་འགྱུར་རོ། །

མི་དགེའི་འབྲས་འདི་རྣམས་ཀྱི་ས་བོན་ནི། །
ལུས་ངག་ཡིད་ཀྱི་ཉེས་སྤྱད་སྤྱོད་ཀྱིས་ནི། །
ཅི་ནས་དེ་རྡུལ་ཙམ་ཡང་མ་མཆིས་པ། །
དེ་ལྟར་ཉིད་ཀྱི་རྩལ་གྱིས་འབད་པར་མཛོད། །

84
If simply seeing pictures of the hells
And hearing, thinking, reading of them scares,
Or making sculpted figures, need we say
How hard to bear the ripened fruit will be?

85
Of all the forms of happiness there are,
The lord is bliss where craving's fully spent.
So too, of all the misery there is,
The pain in Torment Unsurpassed is worst.

86
For one whole day on earth three hundred darts
Might strike you hard and cause you grievous pain,
But that could never illustrate or match
A fraction of the smallest pain in hell.

87
The frightful pains and torments just described
Are lived and felt throughout a billion years.
Until those evil deeds are fully spent
One will not die and shed this life in hell.

88
The seeds of these the fruits of evil deeds
Are sinful acts of body, speech, and mind.
Work hard therefore and muster all your skill
To never stray a hair's breadth into sin.

དུད་འགྲོའི་སྐྱེ་གནས་ན་ཡང་གསོད་པ་དང་། །
བཅིང་དང་བརྡེག་སོགས་སྡུག་བསྔལ་སྣ་ཚོགས་པ། །
ཞི་འགྱུར་དགེ་བ་སྤངས་པ་རྣམས་ལ་ནི། །
གཅིག་ལ་གཅིག་ཟ་ཤིན་ཏུ་མི་བཟད་པ། །

ཁ་ཅིག་མུ་ཏིག་བལ་དང་རུས་པ་དང་། །
ཤ་དང་ལྤགས་པའི་ཆེད་དུ་འཆི་བར་འགྱུར། །
དབང་མེད་གཞན་དག་རྡོག་པ་ལག་པ་དང་། །
ལྕུགས་དང་ལྕུགས་ཀྱུ་གདབ་པས་བཏབ་སྟེ་བཀོལ། །

ཡི་དྭགས་ན་ཡང་འདོད་པས་ཕོངས་པ་ཡིས། །
བསྐྱེད་པའི་སྡུག་བསྔལ་རྒྱུན་ཆགས་མི་འཆོས་པ། །
བཀྲེས་སྐོམ་གྲང་དྲོ་ངལ་དང་འཇིགས་པ་ཡིས། །
བསྐྱེད་པ་ཤིན་ཏུ་མི་བཟད་བསྟེན་འཚལ་ལོ། །

ཁ་ཅིག་ཁ་ནི་ཁབ་ཀྱི་མིག་ཙམ་ལ། །
ལྟོ་བ་རི་ཡི་གཏོས་ཙམ་བཀྲེས་པས་ཉེན། །
མི་གཙང་གྱི་ནར་བོར་བ་ཆུང་ཟད་ཀྱང་། །
འཚལ་བའི་མཐུ་དང་ལྡན་པ་མ་ལགས་སོ། །

ཁ་ཅིག་ལྤགས་རུས་ལུས་ཤིང་གཅེར་བུ་སྟེ། །
ཏ་ལའི་ཡང་སྡོག་བསྐམས་པ་ལྟ་བུ་ལགས། །
ཁ་ཅིག་མཚན་ཞིང་ཁ་ནས་འབར་བ་སྟེ། །
ཟས་སུ་འབར་བའི་ཁར་བབས་བྱེ་མ་འཚལ། །

89
For animals there's multifold distress—
They're slaughtered, tied up, beaten, and the rest.
For those denied the virtue that brings peace
There's agony as one devours another.

90
Some of them are killed just for their pearls,
Their wool, or bones, their meat or skins and fur,
And other helpless beasts are forced to work,
They're kicked or struck with hands, with whips and goads.

91
For pretas too there's not the slightest break
In suffering from their unfulfilled desires.
What dire misery they must endure
From hunger, thirst, cold, heat, fatigue, and fear.

92
Some, their mouths like needles' eyes, their bellies
Huge as mountains, ache from want of food.
They do not even have the strength to eat
Discarded scraps, the smallest bits of filth.

93
Some, their naked bodies skin and bone,
Are like the dried-out tops of tala trees.
And some have mouths that belch forth fire by night:
Into their burning mouths sand falls as food.

སྨད་རིགས་འགའ་ནི་རྣག་དང་ཕྱི་ས་དང་། །
ཁྲག་སོགས་མི་གཙང་བ་ཡང་མི་རྙེད་དེ། །
ཕན་ཚུན་གདོང་དུ་འཚོག་ཅིང་མགྲིན་པ་ནས། །
ལྦ་བ་བྲུང་བ་སྨིན་པའི་རྣག་འཚལ་ལོ། །

ཡི་དྭགས་རྣམས་ལ་སོས་ཀའི་དུས་སུ་ནི། །
ཟླ་བའང་ཚ་ལ་དགུན་ནི་ཉི་མའང་གྲང་། །
ལྗོན་ཤིང་འབྲས་བུ་མེད་འགྱུར་འདི་དག་གིས། །
བལྟས་པ་ཙམ་གྱིས་ཀླུང་ཡང་བསྐམ་པར་འགྱུར། །

བར་ཆད་མེད་པར་སྡུག་བསྔལ་བསྟེན་གྱུར་པ། །
ཉེས་པར་སྤྱོད་པའི་ལས་ཀྱི་ཞགས་པ་ནི། །
སྲ་བས་བཅིངས་པའི་ལུས་ཅན་ཁ་ཅིག་ལོ། །
ལྔ་སྟོང་དག་དང་ཁྲིར་ཡང་འཆིར་མི་འགྱུར། །

དེ་ལྟར་ཡི་དྭགས་རྣམས་ཀྱི་སྣ་ཚོགས་པའི། །
སྡུག་བསྔལ་རོ་གཅིག་ཐོབ་པ་གང་ལགས་པ། །
དེ་ཡི་རྒྱུ་ནི་སྐྱེ་བོ་འཇུངས་དགའ་བ། །
སེར་སྣ་འཕགས་མིན་ལགས་པར་སངས་རྒྱས་གསུངས། །

མཐོ་རིས་ན་ཡང་བདེ་ཆེན་དེ་དག་གི། །
འཆི་འཕོའི་སྡུག་བསྔལ་ཉིད་ནི་དེ་བས་ཆེ། །
དེ་ལྟར་བསམས་ནས་ཡ་རབས་རྣམས་ཀྱིས་ནི། །
ཟད་འགྱུར་མཐོ་རིས་སླད་དུ་སྲེད་མི་བགྱི། །

94
A few unlucky ones don't even find
Some dirt to eat—pus, excrement, or blood.
They hit each other in the face and eat
The pus that festers from their swollen necks.

95
For hungry ghosts the summer moon's too hot,
In wintertime the sun is far too cold,
Fine trees in orchards wilt and lose their fruit,
And simply from their gaze great streams run dry.

96
And some have bodies bound by that tight noose,
Their karmic store of previous evil deeds,
Now borne as constant misery and pain;
For five, ten thousand years they will not die.

97
The cause of these the pretas' varied woes
And all such kindred torments one might get
Is being greedy, this the Buddha said:
Stinginess is not for the sublime.

98
Even in the higher realms the pains of death
Are more intense than is their greatest bliss.
And so good people who reflect on this
Don't crave the higher realms, which soon must end.

ལུས་ཀྱི་ཁ་དོག་མི་སྡུག་འགྱུར་བ་དང་། །
སྟན་ལ་མི་དགའ་མེ་ཏོག་ཕྲེང་རྙིང་དང་། །
གོས་ལ་དྲི་མ་ཆགས་དང་ལུས་ལ་ནི། །
སྔོན་ཆད་མེད་པའི་རྔུལ་འབྱུང་ཞེས་བགྱི་བ། །

མཐོ་རིས་འཆི་འཕོ་སྟོན་བགྱིད་འཆི་ལྟས་ལྔ། །
ལྷ་ཡུལ་གནས་པའི་ལྷ་རྣམས་ལ་འབྱུང་སྟེ། །
ས་སྟེང་མི་རྣམས་འཆི་བར་འགྱུར་བ་དག །
སྟོན་པར་བྱེད་པའི་འཆི་ལྟས་རྣམས་དང་འདྲ། །

ལྷ་ཡི་འཇིག་རྟེན་དག་ནས་འཕོས་པ་ལ། །
གལ་ཏེ་དགེ་བའི་ལྷག་མ་འགའ་མེད་ན། །
དེ་ནས་དབང་མེད་དུད་འགྲོ་ཡི་དྭགས་དང་། །
དམྱལ་བར་གནས་པ་གང་ཡང་རུང་བར་འགྱུར། །

ལྷ་མིན་དག་ནའང་རང་བཞིན་གྱིས་ལྷ་ཡི། །
དཔལ་ལ་སྡང་ཕྱིར་ཡིད་ཀྱི་སྡུག་བསྔལ་ཆེ། །
དེ་དག་བློ་དང་ལྡན་ཡང་འགྲོ་བ་ཡི། །
སྒྲིབ་པས་བདེན་པ་མཐོང་བ་མ་མཆིས་སོ། །

འཁོར་བ་དེ་འདྲ་ལགས་པས་ལྷ་མི་དང་། །
དམྱལ་བ་ཡི་དྭགས་འདུད་འགྲོ་རྣམས་དག་ཏུ། །
སྐྱེ་བ་བཟང་པོ་མ་ལགས་སྐྱེ་བ་ནི། །
གནོད་པ་དུ་མའི་སྣོད་གྱུར་ལགས་པར་མཁྱེན་མཛོད། །

99
Their bodies' colors cease to charm and please,
Their seats grow hard, their flowered wreaths do wilt,
Their clothes are stained, and on their bodies now appear
Rank drops of sweat they never had before.

100
These five are signs that herald death in heaven,
Appearing to the gods in their abodes.
They're not unlike the signs of death that warn
Of coming death in humans on the earth.

101
Those gods who transmigrate from heavenly worlds
And do not have some little virtue left
Will tumble, helpless, to their just abodes
As beasts or hungry spirits or in hell.

102
The asuras begrudge the gods their splendor,
Their inbred loathing thus torments their minds.
Though clever, they're obscured as all their kind,
And so it is they cannot see the truth.

103
Samsara is like this, and thus we are reborn
As gods, as humans, denizens in hell,
As ghosts or animals; but you should know
That birth's not good, a pot of many ills.

མགོ་འམ་གོས་ལ་གློ་བུར་མེ་ཞོར་ན། །
དེ་དག་བཟློག་ཕྱིར་བགྱི་བ་བཏང་ནས་ཀྱང་། །
ཡང་སྲིད་མེད་པར་བགྱི་སླད་འབད་འཚལ་ཏེ། །
དེ་བས་ཆེས་མཆོག་དགོས་པ་གཞན་མ་མཆིས། །

ཚུལ་ཁྲིམས་དག་དང་བསམ་གཏན་ཤེས་རབ་ཀྱིས། །
མྱ་ངན་འདས་ཞི་དུལ་བ་དྲི་མེད་པའི། །
གོ་འཕང་མི་རྒ་མི་འཆི་ཟད་མི་འཚལ། །
ས་ཆུ་མེ་རླུང་ཉི་ཟླ་བྲལ་ཐོབ་མཛོད། །

དྲན་དང་ཆོས་རབ་འབྱེད་དང་བརྩོན་འགྲུས་དང་། །
དགའ་དང་ཤིན་ཏུ་སྦྱངས་དང་ཏིང་འཛིན་དང་། །
བཏང་སྙོམས་འདི་བདུན་བྱང་ཆུབ་ཡན་ལག་སྟེ། །
མྱ་ངན་འདས་ཐོབ་བགྱིད་པའི་དགེ་ཚོགས་ལགས། །

ཤེས་རབ་མེད་པར་བསམ་གཏན་ཡོད་མིན་ཏེ། །
བསམ་གཏན་མེད་པར་ཡང་ནི་ཤེས་རབ་མེད། །
གང་ལ་དེ་གཉིས་ཡོད་པ་སྲིད་པ་ཡི། །
རྒྱ་མཚོ་གནག་རྗེས་ལྟ་བུར་འཚལ་བར་བགྱི། །

ལུང་མ་བསྟན་པ་བཅུ་བཞི་འཇིག་རྟེན་ན། །
ཉི་མའི་གཉེན་གྱིས་རབ་གསུངས་གང་དག་ལགས། །
དེ་དག་རྣམས་ལ་བསམ་པར་མི་བགྱི་སྟེ། །
དེ་ཡིས་བློ་ནི་ཞི་བར་བགྱིད་མ་ལགས། །

104
Give up your efforts trying to stop all this
As if your hair or clothes had just caught fire;
Just do your best to not be born again:
No greater goal or need is there than this.

105
With discipline and concentration, wisdom too,
Attain nirvana, peaceful, disciplined, immaculate,
Unageing, deathless, inexhaustible, and quite distinct
From earth and water, fire, wind, sun, and moon.

106
Mindfulness, discernment, diligence, a joyful mind,
And flexibility, concentration, evenness—
These seven limbs are elements that lead to Buddhahood,
They gather virtue and attain the state beyond all pain.

107
Lacking wisdom, concentration fails,
And without concentration, wisdom too.
For someone who has both, samsara's sea
Fills no more than the print left by a hoof.

108
The Kinsman of the Sun did well pronounce
With silence on the fourteen worldly points.
On these you must not ponder or reflect,
With them your mind will never be at peace.

མ་རིག་པ་ལས་ལས་ཏེ་དེ་ལས་ནི། །
རྣམ་ཤེས་དེ་ལས་མིང་དང་གཟུགས་རབ་འབྱུང་། །
དེ་ལས་སྐྱེ་མཆེད་དྲུག་སྟེ་དེ་ལས་ནི། །
རེག་པ་ཀུན་ཏུ་འབྱུང་བར་ཐུབ་པས་གསུངས། །

རེག་པ་ལས་ནི་ཚོར་བ་ཀུན་འབྱུང་སྟེ། །
ཚོར་བའི་གཞི་ལས་སྲེད་པ་འབྱུང་བར་འགྱུར། །
སྲེད་ལས་ལེན་པ་སྐྱེ་བར་འགྱུར་བ་སྟེ། །
དེ་ལས་སྲིད་པ་སྲིད་ལས་སྐྱེ་བ་ལགས། །

སྐྱེ་བ་ཡོད་ན་མྱ་ངན་ན་ན་རྒ་དང་། །
འདོད་པས་ཕོངས་དང་འཆི་དང་འཇིག་སོགས་ཀྱིས། །
སྡུག་བསྔལ་ཕུང་པོ་ཤིན་ཏུ་ཆེ་འབྱུང་སྟེ། །
སྐྱེ་བ་འགགས་པས་འདི་ཀུན་འགག་པར་འགྱུར། །

རྟེན་ཅིང་འབྲེལ་བར་འབྱུང་འདི་རྒྱལ་བ་ཡི། །
གསུང་གི་མཛོད་ཀྱི་གཅེས་པ་ཟབ་མོ་སྟེ། །
གང་གིས་འདི་ནི་ཡང་དག་མཐོང་བ་དེས། །
སངས་རྒྱས་དེ་ཉིད་རིག་པ་རྣམ་མཆོག་མཐོང་། །

ཡང་དག་ལྟ་དང་འཚོ་དང་རྩོལ་བ་དང་། །
དྲན་དང་ཏིང་འཛིན་ངག་དང་ལས་མཐའ་དང་། །
ཡང་དག་རྟོག་ཉིད་ལམ་གྱི་ཡན་ལག་བརྒྱད། །
འདི་ནི་ཞི་བར་བགྱི་སླད་བསྒོམ་པར་བགྱི། །

109
From ignorance comes action, and from that
Comes consciousness, thence name-and-form appears.
From that arise the six sense faculties,
Whence contact comes, thus did the Buddha teach.

110
And then from contact feeling comes to be,
And based on feeling, craving will appear.
Again from craving grasping will be born,
And then becoming, and from this there's birth.

111
Then once there's birth, comes misery untold,
And sickness, ageing, wants frustrated, death,
Decay, in short the whole great mass of pain.
If birth is stopped, all this will be no more.

112
Within the treasury of Buddha's words
There's none so precious, so profound as this.
And those who see that things dependently arise
Do see the Buddha, perfect knower of the truth.

113
Perfect view and livelihood, with effort,
Mindfulness and concentration, perfect speech,
And conduct, perfect thought—the path's eight limbs—
To find true peace, please meditate on these.

སྐྱེ་འདི་སྡུག་བསྔལ་སྲིད་པ་ཞེས་བགྱི་བ། །
དེ་ནི་དེ་ཡི་ཀུན་འབྱུང་རྒྱ་ཆེན་ཏེ། །
འདི་འགོག་པ་ནི་ཐར་པ་ལགས་ཏེ་དེ། །
འཐོབ་བགྱིད་འཕགས་ལམ་ཡན་ལག་དེ་བརྒྱད་ལགས། །

དེ་ལྟར་འཕགས་པའི་བདེན་པ་བཞི་པོ་དག། །
མཐོང་བར་བགྱི་སླད་རྟག་ཏུ་བརྩོན་པར་བགྱི། །
པང་ན་དཔལ་གནས་ཁྱིམ་པ་རྣམས་ཀྱིས་ཀྱང་། །
ཤེས་པས་ཉོན་མོངས་ཆུ་བོ་ལས་བརྒལ་གྱི། །

གང་དག་ཆོས་མངོན་བགྱིས་པ་དེ་དག་ཀྱང་། །
གནམ་ལས་བབས་པ་མ་ལགས་ལོ་ཏོག་བཞིན། །
ས་རུམ་ནས་འཐོན་མ་ལགས་དེ་དག་སྟོན། །
ཉོན་མོངས་རག་ལས་སོ་སོའི་སྐྱེ་བོར་བས། །

བསླེངས་དང་བྲལ་ལ་ཧ་ཅང་མང་ཅི་འཚལ། །
ཕན་པའི་གདམས་ངག་དོན་པོ་འདི་ལགས་ཏེ། །
ཁྱོད་ཀྱིས་ཐུགས་དུལ་མཛོད་ཅིག་བཅོམ་ལྡན་གྱིས། །
སེམས་ནི་ཆོས་ཀྱི་རྩ་བ་ལགས་པར་གསུངས། །

ཁྱོད་ལ་དེ་སྐད་གདམས་པ་གང་ལགས་དེ། །
བས་པར་དགེ་སློང་གིས་ཀྱང་བགྱི་བར་དཀའ། །
འདི་ལས་གང་ཞིག་སྤྱོད་པའི་ངོ་བོ་དེའི། །
ཡོན་ཏན་བསྟེན་པས་སྐུ་ཚེ་དོན་ཡོད་མཛོད། །

114
To take birth is to suffer, and to crave
Is its immense and universal source.
Make craving cease and freedom will be yours,
To achieve that take the Eightfold Noble Path.

115
For you to see these same Four Noble Truths
You must strive hard to practice constantly.
Even worldly men with fortune in their laps,
Through knowledge, crossed that river, troubled states;

116
And even those who realized the truth
Did not fall from the heavens, nor emerge
Like crops of corn from earth's dark depths, but once
Were ruled by kleshas and were ordinary men.

117
O Fearless One, what need to tell you more?
For here's the counsel that will truly help:
The vital point is tame your mind, for mind's
The root of Dharma, so the Buddha said.

118
It's hard enough for monks to follow perfectly
All these instructions that I've given you.
Yet practice excellence, the very pith
Of one of these, and give your life its sense.

ཀུན་གྱི་དགེ་བ་ཀུན་ལ་ཡི་རང་ཞིང་། །
ཉིད་ཀྱིས་ལེགས་པར་སྤྱད་པ་རྣམ་གསུམ་ཡང་། །
སངས་རྒྱས་ཉིད་ཐོབ་བགྱི་སླད་ཡོངས་བསྔོས་ནས། །
དེ་ནས་དགེ་བའི་ཕུང་པོ་འདི་ཡིས་ནི། །

སྐྱེ་བ་དཔག་ཏུ་མེད་པར་ལྷ་མི་ཡི། །
འཇིག་རྟེན་ཀུན་གྱི་རྣལ་འབྱོར་དབང་མཛད་ནས། །
འཕགས་པ་སྤྱན་རས་གཟིགས་དབང་སྤྱོད་པ་ཡིས། །
འགྲོ་བ་ཉམས་ཐག་མང་པོ་རྗེས་བཟུང་སྟེ། །

འབྲུངས་ནས་ནད་རྒ་འདོད་ཆགས་ཞེ་སྡང་རྣམས། །
བསལ་ཏེ་སངས་རྒྱས་ཞིང་དུ་བཅོམ་ལྡན་འདས། །
འོད་དཔག་མེད་དང་འདྲ་བར་འཇིག་རྟེན་གྱི། །
མགོན་པོ་སྐུ་ཚེ་དཔག་ཏུ་མེད་པར་མཛོད། །

ཤེས་རབ་ཚུལ་ཁྲིམས་གཏོང་འབྱུང་གྲགས་ཆེན་དྲི་མ་མེད། །
ལྷ་ཡུལ་ནམ་མཁའ་དང་ནི་ས་སྟེང་རྒྱས་བརྗོད་ནས། །
ས་ལ་མི་དང་མཐོ་རིས་ལྷ་ནི་ན་ཆུང་མཆོག །
བདེ་དགས་དགའ་བ་ངེས་པར་རབ་ཏུ་ཞི་མཛད་དོ། །

ཉོན་མོངས་ཉམ་ཐག་སེམས་ཅན་ཚོགས་ཀྱི་འཇིགས་སྐྱེ་དང་། །
འཆི་བ་ཞི་མཛད་རྒྱལ་བའི་དབང་པོ་ཉིད་བརྙེས་ནས། །
འཇིག་རྟེན་ལས་འདས་མིང་ཙམ་ཞི་ལ་མི་བསྙེངས་པ། །
མི་འགྲེས་ནོངས་པ་མི་མངའི་གོ་འཕང་བརྙེས་པར་མཛོད།

119
Rejoicing in the virtuous deeds of all,
Now dedicate your three good kinds of acts
To all that they may come to Buddhahood.
Then by this mass of virtuous deeds may you,

120
In boundless lives in worlds of gods and men,
Be master of the yoga of all excellence,
And like Sublime Chenrezig, may you work
To guide the many feeble, stricken souls.

121
And thus may you take many rebirths and dispel all ills,
Old age, desire, and hatred in a perfect Buddhafield.
May you have infinite life, as a Protector of the World
Like Buddha Amitabha, Sublime Lord of Boundless Light.

122
And springing from your wisdom, discipline, and bounty, may your fame
And stainless virtues spread throughout the gods' realms, in the sky
And on the earth, and may you firmly quell the carefree ways
Of gods and men whose sole delight and joy is pretty girls.

123
And once you've reached the Mighty Buddha state, removing fear
And birth and death for hosts of stricken and afflicted souls,
Then let mere name be stilled, beyond the world, and reach
The never-changing level, free from fear, that knows no wrong.

བཤེས་པའི་སྤྲིང་ཡིག་སློབ་དཔོན་འཕགས་པ་ཀླུ་སྒྲུབ་ཀྱིས་མཛའ་བོ་རྒྱལ་པོ་བདེ་སྤྱོད་ལ་བསྐུར་བ་རྫོགས་སོ། །

རྒྱ་གར་གྱི་མཁན་པོ་སརྦ་ཛྙཱ་ན་དེ་ཝ་དང་། ཞུ་ཆེན་གྱི་ལོ་ཙཱ་བ་བན་དེ་དཔལ་བརྩེགས་ཀྱིས་བསྒྱུར་ཅིང་ཞུས་ཏེ་གཏན་ལ་ཕབ་པའོ།།

This completes the *Letter to a Friend* written by the Sublime Master Nagarjuna to a friend, King Surabhibhadra. It was translated, corrected, and authenticated by the learned Indian abbot Sarvajñanadeva and the great reviser and translator Venerable Paltsek.

Kangyur Rinpoche's Commentary on the *Letter to a Friend*

Kangyur Rinpoche (1897–1975)

Here is an explanation of the *Letter to a Friend* by the glorious protector Arya Nagarjuna. It has three parts: a virtuous beginning, the introduction; a virtuous middle, the actual text; and a virtuous end, the conclusion.

Part One

INTRODUCTION

I. The Title

A. The Indian title

In Sanskrit: Suhrillekha

Of the many different regions of India there were six great regions in which the Buddha's doctrine spread, as we can read in *The Flower Garland of the Vinaya*:

Six great cities are there and well known:
Shravasti and Shakata,
Champaka and Varanasi,
Vaishali and Rajagriha.

In these regions there were three hundred and sixty different languages spoken, of which the most important were the four major languages: Ababramsha, the descriptive language of the common people; Prakrit, the evolved language of the lowest classes;[1] Pishacha, the language of ogres and spirits; and Sanskrit, the language of the gods. Foremost among these is the divine language of Sanskrit, for it was the language in which all the enlightened beings who came in the past taught, it will be used by all those who teach in the future, and it is therefore the basic language used by all those who teach at present. It is this language that is referred to by **In the language of India: Suhrillekha**, indicating the Indian title.

B. The Tibetan title

In Tibetan: bshes pa'i spring yig

This title translated into the pure **language of Tibet** is **bshes pa'i spring yig** (meaning *Letter to a Friend*).[2]

C. The correspondence between the two languages
Suhrid means "friend" (*bshes pa*), *lekha* means "letter" (*spring yig*).

D. A commentary on the meaning of the title
The *Letter to a Friend* consists of advice in the form of an epistle from Nagarjuna to a king with whom he was friendly. When Arya Nagarjuna was on his way to the northern continent of Uttarakuru he saw several children playing. Reading the palm of one of them, he predicted that he would become a king. By the time he arrived back in India from Uttarakuru, the child had become a ruler, with the name Surabhibhadra. It is to him that this letter was addressed.[3]

II. The Translator's Homage

Homage to the Gentle and Glorious Youth (Mañjugosha).

The translator's homage is the "homage made at the Dharma King's command," since it is made in accordance with the edicts established by the Dharma King Tri Relpachen. And it is the "homage that identifies the pitaka" since it serves to identify the corresponding pitaka. In the Vinaya and related texts it is "I pay homage to the Omniscient One"; in the Sutras and related texts it is "I pay homage to all the Buddhas and Bodhisattvas"; and in the Abhidharma and related texts it is "I pay homage to Arya Mañjugosha."

This particular text is related to the Abhidharma and so here homage is paid to Arya Mañjugosha, "Gentle and Glorious Youth." He is **Gentle and Glorious** because he leads beings very gently along the path of the Great Vehicle, in stages, using the wisdom of the two kinds of knowledge concerning the aspects of elimination and realization on the path, benefiting everyone in whichever way is appropriate, and whatever their philosophical leanings, Buddhist or non-Buddhist. And he is **Youth** because though he is the father who has begotten countless Buddhas, he remains youthful.

The translator's **homage** was made by the great translator Kawa Paltsek, as he began translating this shastra into Tibetan, with great respect—physically, verbally, and mentally. Its purpose was to ensure that the translation would be completed and that there would be no obstacles to the work of translation.[4]

Part Two

THE ACTUAL TEXT

The actual text also has a beginning, middle, and end—prologue, explanation of the main text, and epilogue.

I. Prologue

A. Using the commitment to compose the text as an exhortation to listen

> Listen now to these few lines of noble song
> That I've composed for those with many virtues, fit for good,
> To help them yearn for merit springing from
> The sacred words of He Who's Gone to Bliss. (1)

For those who **naturally have good qualities**, that is, who have formerly accumulated positive deeds, which are the causes of temporary and ultimate excellence, and who are worthy vessels for practicing positive actions and are therefore **fit for virtue**, **I**, Nagarjuna, **have composed a few** verses put together using **the** style of composition known as **sublime melody.**[5] Their subject is the Dharma **whose source is the** Excellent **Words**[6] or **declarations of the Sugata.** My purpose in composing them is that I myself or others might **aspire to merit**, for it is said,

> *All things are conditions,*
> *They depend on what one wishes.*

They are worth your listening to, O King.

B. A lesson in humility and why one should listen

1. Humility with regard to the words

> The wise will always honor and bow down
> To Buddha statues, though they're made of wood;
> So too, although these lines of mine be poor,
> Do not feel scorn, they teach the Holy Way. (2)

One might think that since the Mighty One taught everything for attaining the higher realms and the lasting happiness of liberation and omniscience there is no need for this teaching. But **just as the wise venerate a statue of the Sugata, whatever** the quality of the material, **whether it is made of** some base material such as stone or **wood** or of a superior substance such as gold, **in the same way, however** excellent or **poor** these lines—**my poetry**—may be, their subject is how to reach the higher realms and the lasting happiness of liberation and omniscience, and **they follow the teaching of the holy Dharma,** which shows that. **For that reason**, to the wise, who rely not on words but on the meaning, they are worth praising; **they are not to be despised** but are worth listening to and putting into practice.

2. Humility with regard to the meaning

> While you have surely learned and understood
> The Mighty Buddha's many lovely words,
> Is it not so that something made of chalk
> By moonlight lit shines gleaming whiter still? (3)

Although you, O King, **may well have absorbed the Mahamuni's many pleasant**, beautiful, and excellent **words** by listening to them and reflecting on them, nevertheless, as it will help make their meaning even clearer, this letter is still worthy of your attention. Take the example of a fine house that has been whitewashed with **chalk**: although it is naturally white, **the light of the moon at midnight** striking it **makes it even more intensely white, does it not?**

II. The Main Text

A. Faith as a support on the path to the higher realms and lasting happiness

1. Brief account of six things one should keep in mind, the Buddha and so forth, which are the basis of faith

> Six things there are the Buddhas have explained,
> And all their virtues you must keep in mind:
> The Buddha, Dharma, Sangha, bounteous acts,
> And moral laws and gods—each one recall. (4)

The Victorious Ones have perfectly explained six things to be kept in mind. Keep in mind the **Buddha**, the Buddha Bhagavan who is Thus Gone and so forth. Keep in mind the **Dharma**, the Bhagavan's teaching that is excellently spoken and so forth. Keep in mind the **Sangha**, the Bhagavan's Sangha of Shravakas who abide excellently and so forth.[7] Keep in mind **bounteousness**, untainted by miserliness and so forth. Keep in mind **discipline**, unspoiled, free of faults, unadulterated, unobscured, the discipline that accomplishes the concentration praised by the wise. And keep in mind **celestial beings**, the gods of the realm of the Four Great Kings, and those from the Heaven of the Thirty-Three up to "Mastery over Others' Creations," and so on, who constitute the particular result of practicing the teachings for attaining the higher realms. **Keep in mind the many virtues of each of these,** as they have been described in the sutras.

2. Detailed explanation of the last three things to be kept in mind

a. Keeping celestial beings in mind

> With body, speech, and mind always rely
> On wholesome deeds, the tenfold virtuous path.
> Avoiding liquor at all costs, thus find
> True joy to lead a life of virtuous deeds. (5)

Because it is the nature of the **positive** act of concentration to lead to a pleasant result, such **actions** constitute the path that leads to happy rebirth.[8] **You should** therefore **constantly rely on the tenfold path**, performing the ten positive actions while avoiding the ten negative actions—the three **physical** acts of taking life, taking what is not given, and sexual misconduct; the four **verbal** acts of lying, sowing discord, harsh speech, and worthless chatter; and the three **mental** acts of covetousness, wishing harm on others, and wrong views. And because they cause carelessness, **abstain from intoxicants** in all circumstances. **In this way, take joy in a life of virtue**, without being careless and harming others.

b. Keeping bounteousness in mind

> Possessions are ephemeral and essenceless—
> Know this and give them generously to monks,
> To brahmins, to the poor, and to your friends:
> Beyond there is no greater friend than gift. (6)

Having realized that possessions such as food are inconstant and **fluctuate**, that in changing and transforming they **are devoid of essence**, in order to make them meaningful[9] **try to use them properly, giving to** those with good qualities (**monks and brahmins**), to those who suffer (**the poor**, the sick, and so forth), to those who help you (**friends**) and to those you venerate (spiritual teachers and parents).[10] Even **beyond** the world **there is no friend more sublime**, more beneficial, **than giving**, because it gives rise directly and indirectly to ripened effects that are inexhaustible.

c. Keeping discipline in mind

> Keep your vows unbroken, undegraded,
> Uncorrupted, and quite free of stain.
> Just as the earth's the base for all that's still or moves,
> On discipline, it's said, is founded all that's good. (7)

Your discipline should have four particular features. In not transgressing the basic precepts it should be **unbroken**. In not transgressing the most minor branches it should be **without degradation**—this is the old sense of the term in Tibetan and means "unstained by faults and therefore vast and elevated." It should be **unadulterated** by anything incompatible, and it should be **untainted** by selfish thoughts or wishing to better one's lot. **Observe all these. Just as the earth** supports **things moving and unmoving**—beings and trees, for instance—**discipline is the foundation of all**

good qualities, concentration, wisdom, and so forth, as our Teacher, the Buddha, has **declared**: reliance on discipline gives rise to concentration and therefore naturally gives rise to meditation.

B. The essence of the path

1. Brief introduction

> Generosity and discipline, patience, diligence,
> Concentration, and the wisdom that knows thusness—
> Those measureless perfections, make them grow,
> And be a Mighty Conqueror who's crossed samsara's sea. (8)

Develop within you **the** six **transcendent perfections, which cannot be fathomed** by the Shravakas and Pratyekabuddhas: unstinting **generosity** reinforced by bodhichitta and wisdom; **discipline**—the avoidance of negative actions and their basis, attachment and so forth; the **patience** to put up with difficulties; **diligence**—delight in positive actions; one-pointed **concentration** on virtue and on the absolute; **and wisdom**, the knowledge of **thusness**, the ultimate meaning, just as it is. And **be the Mighty Victor who**, as the result of doing so, **has reached the other side of the ocean of existence**. Here Nagarjuna is saying that since one will become a Mighty Buddha through these six transcendent perfections, one should make them part of one's being.

2. Detailed explanation: the six transcendent perfections

a. Generosity

> Those who show their parents great respect
> With Brahma or a Master will be linked;
> By venerating them they'll win repute,
> In future they'll attain the higher realms. (9)

The kind of person who respectfully **makes offerings to** his **parents** is unharmed by nonhumans and blessed by the gods, and is therefore **to be associated with Brahma**, worthy of the world's offerings. And because he has the teacher's blessings **he is also to be associated with a master** who teaches the essential point of what to do and what to give up. Besides these advantages, it is good **to make offerings to them**, one's parents, for **one will have a good reputation** even in this life, **and in the hereafter**, that is, in the next life **too, one will attain the higher realms**. So apply yourself to venerating your parents and others.

b. Discipline

i. Precepts that have to be kept

> Eschew all harm, don't steal, make love, or lie,
> Abstain from drink, untimely greed for food,
> Indulging in high beds, and singing too,
> Refrain from dancing, all adornments shun. (10)
>
> For men and women who keep this eight-branched vow
> And emulate the vows the Arhats took,
> Their wish to nurture and to cleanse will grant
> Them handsome bodies as celestial gods. (11)

These concern laypeople. **Abstain** for twenty-four hours **from the following various acts**: killing, or here, **harming**, other living beings; **theft**—that is, taking what is not given; **sexual intercourse** ("impure conduct");[11] telling **lies** (in particular, claiming to have sublime qualities one does not have);[12] **drinking alcohol**, which produces a careless state of intoxication; **greedily eating at inappropriate times**; **indulging in a bed high**er than eighteen inches; the three activities of **singing**, **dancing** (along with dressing up), and playing music; and these three: wearing **necklaces** of jewels and other ornaments that are a source of vanity, wearing multicolored ornaments, and using sweet smelling perfumes and so forth.

As a result of their **desire to nurture** the seed of positive actions and **purify** negative actions, **men and women**—that is, those on the three continents where they can observe such discipline[13]—who **keep these eight branches** with renewal and confession,[14] **following the example of the discipline of Arhats** in the past, **are granted** (and obtain) a **pleasing body** in the six realms **of the gods of enjoyment**.[15]

ii. Getting rid of incompatible traits

> Stinginess and cunning, greed and sloth
> And arrogance, attachment, hate, and pride
> ("I've breeding, good looks, learning, youth, and power")—
> Such traits are seen as enemies of good. (12)

Consider the following traits **as enemies**, since they destroy **positive actions**: **niggardliness** with regard to one's own possessions; **craftiness** in skillfully playing down one's own defects, and deceitfulness in pretending to have certain qualities so as to beguile others; **attachment** to body and wealth; **laziness**, that is, not delighting in virtue; **arrogance**, thinking one has qualities that one does not have; **desire**—craving for existence; **hatred**—the hatred of the inhabitants of the Hell of Torment Unsurpassed; and **pride**—being proud of one's **breeding** ("I am superior," one thinks), proud of one's **physique**, proud of one's **learning**, proud of one's youthfulness ("I've lost none of my **youthfulness**, I'm still in top form."), and proud of one's power ("How **immensely powerful** I am!").

iii. Exercising carefulness regarding what is compatible with discipline

> Carefulness is the way to deathlessness,
> While carelessness is death, the Buddha taught.
> And thus, so that your virtuous deeds may grow,
> Be careful, constantly and with respect. (13)

Carefulness is characterized by practicing virtuous activities and guarding the mind from tainted activities. As **the Capable One has taught** in such passages as this one from the sutras, it is the **way** beyond suffering, like **the nectar of immortality**:

> *Carefulness is the way of immortality,*
> *Carelessness is the way of death.*
> *With carefulness one will not perish,*
> *With carelessness one always dies.*

Carelessness becomes the **way** to experiencing the suffering **of** birth and **death** in samsara. This is widely demonstrated in sutras such as the *Sutra of Sublime Dharma of Clear Recollection*:

Humans who have fortune won,
Who do not act with carelessness,
Are called "the wise," for thus they are,
Their opposites are otherwise.
The gods, seduced by carelessness,
Will swiftly be reborn in hell.
And so, O you who are truly wise,
Treat carelessness like poisoned food.

Further on we read:

From evil deeds quite free, rely
On a mind that's free from carelessness:
'Tis there a grove of utter peace,
The realm in which the yogis dwell.

And again:

Use every method to eliminate
The poison that is carelessness.
Those who are free from carelessness
Will cross the oceanlike three worlds.

Accordingly, so that you might give birth to **virtuous ways** where you have not done so, and where you have conceived them **develop** them more and more, **respectfully practice carefulness**, habituating yourself **all the time** to virtuous activities.

iv. Benefits and examples of being careful

Those who formerly were careless
But then took heed are beautiful and fair,
As is the moon emerging from the clouds,
Like Nanda, Angulimala, Darshaka, Udayana. (14)

One might wonder whether there is any point in instructing those who have been careless in the past. Some people, however, **having previously been careless** (indulging without thinking in negative actions as a result of their being dominated by afflictive emotions or influenced by evil companions), **subsequently**, on meeting a spiritual friend and wholeheartedly adopting what is right and abandoning wrong, **become careful.** Such people, as we can see from the following examples, **are like the moon unobscured by the clouds—utterly beautiful**.

Nanda was a randy young Shakya, a younger brother of the Buddha. He could not part from his wife for a single instant. He took ordination in the Buddha's doctrine but still thought longingly about his wife, day and night, and thus failed to practice virtue. The Buddha, seeing that he would be reborn in the hells, instructed him personally. As a result Nanda became afraid, started practicing the path, and attained the level of Arhat. He was commended by the Buddha as the Shravaka who had most successfully controlled his senses.

Angulimala[16] was the gullible son of a brahmin. His teacher deceitfully instructed him, "If you kill a thousand people and make a garland of their fingers, you will go to the celestial abodes." He had slain all but one of the thousand when the Buddha ordained him and taught him the Dharma. He became an Arhat.

Then there is the example of **Darshaka**, another name for Ajatashatru. Having met his companion in evil, Devadatta, he committed a large number of negative actions, among them murdering his father, the king, who was a follower of the Dharma. Later he gained faith in the Buddha, was freed from the results of his negative actions, and became an Arhat.

Udayana[17] killed his mother when she prevented him sleeping with someone else's wife. He took ordination, but when it was realized that he had committed a "crime with immediate retribution,"[18] he was expelled by the Sangha and went to a remote region. He built a temple and stayed there. In due course a large number of monks in the area gathered there, he became their Elder and properly cared for the Sangha. As a result, when he died he had but a "yo-yo"[19] rebirth in hell as the fully ripened effect of his crime with immediate retribution and was then reborn as a god, attaining the result of a Stream Enterer on the Buddha's path.

c. Patience

i. Giving up anger (as a cause)[20]

> Hard to practice, patience knows no peer,
> So never allow yourself a moment's rage.
> Avoid all anger and you will become
> A Non-Returner, so the Buddha said. (15)

There is no other **difficult practice equal to patience**—not getting angry with someone who harms you, and even if you do get angry, not remaining so. It is the ultimate austerity. **Therefore do not allow yourself** even the slightest **occasion for anger**, which is incompatible with such a sublime austerity as patience. Should you wonder why, **the Buddha himself declared that by** being patient and **avoiding getting angry one will attain the** ultimate result of **Non-Returner**, as we find in one of the sutras:

> *Monks, rid yourselves of anger, and thus attest to Non-Return.*

ii. Giving up resentment (as a result)[21]

> "He's abused me, struck, defeated me,
> And all my money too he has purloined!"
> To harbor such resentment leads to strife;
> Give up your grudge and sleep will easily come. (16)

By harboring resentment—"He insulted me with abusive language, **he hit** me with things like stones and sticks, he **got the better of me** by ridiculing me and using his power, **he ran off with my money"**—one builds up the motives for negative actions, physical and verbal, thereby **sparking off disputes**. **By abandoning grudges** one will gain the temporary result[22] of a mind free of anguish and so **fall asleep happily**. *The Way of the Bodhisattva* sums this up as follows:

> *Men of anger have no joy*
> *Forsaken by all happiness and peace.*

and,

But those who seize and crush their anger down
Will find their joy in this and future lives.[23]

iii. In connection with this, a particular feature of the mind that is the basis for patience

Understand your thoughts to be like figures drawn
On water, sandy soil, or carved in stone.
Of these, for tainted thoughts the first's the best,
While when you long for Dharma, it's the last. (17)

Of all the various constant and inconstant mental activities that different kinds of sentient beings can have, you should **know that thoughts are like figures drawn on water**, which instantly dissolve, **or** like drawings on **sand**, which are erased by different conditions, **or** like figures drawn on **stone**, which are indelible. Where thoughts, either positive or negative, are like drawings on sand, this is of medium value. **Of these** three cases, **the first**, where the thoughts are inconstant like figures traced on water, is the **best** as regards **emotionally tainted** thoughts. **As regards aspirations** to undertake **Dharma** practice, **the last**, where the thoughts are stable like figures drawn on stone, is the best. So practice accordingly.

iv. Avoiding harsh words, the main condition that sparks off anger

Three kinds of speech are used by humankind,
And these the Victor variously described:
Like honey, sweet; like flowers, true; like filth,
Improper speech—the last of these eschew. (18)

The Victorious One who has overcome evil ways spoke of three kinds of speech in human beings, namely, sweet, **pleasing** words, **truth,** and **improper speech. Of these three kinds of speech that people use**, the first, **he said**, delights, **like honey**; the second is beautiful and worthy of praise, like **a flower**; the last, because it is to be despised, is like **filth**. Accordingly, **avoid the last of these**, and make good use of the first two.

d. Diligence

i. What one should be diligent in

> Some there are who go from light to light,
> And some whose end from dark is darkness still,
> While some from light to dark, or dark to light
> End up, thus four, of these be as the first. (19)

There are four kinds of individual. Those who go **from** the **light** of the higher realms and again **end up in** the **light** of the higher realms of gods and humans. Those who go **from** the **darkness** of the lower realms and **end up in darkness,** being again reborn in the lower realms. Those who go **from** the **light** of birth in the higher realms to **end up in darkness** as the most wretched of humans or as beings in the three lower realms. And those who go **from** the **darkness** of the three lower realms and wretched states to **end up in** the **light** of the higher realms. **Of these four kinds of individual, you should be the first**, the one who goes from light to light.

ii. An instruction on diligence in matching intention and application

> Men, like mangoes, can be sour and yet look ripe,
> Some though ripe look green, and others green
> Are sour indeed, while others still look ripe
> And ripe they are: from this know how to act. (20)

Human beings are like the fruit of the mango tree. Some **seem ripe**—their actual deeds are wholesome—**but are unripe**—their intention is base. Some **seem unripe**—their deeds are base—**but** in fact **are ripe**—the intention is wholesome. Others **look unripe and are unripe**—both intention and deed are unwholesome. **Yet others look ripe and are ripe**—both intention and deed are wholesome. Knowing the meaning of each of these four characteristics, **whatever you do** you should **gain** a proper **understanding** of the essential point of avoiding and adopting.[24] The last of these four cases is the greatest ally in performing positive actions.

e. Concentration

i. Preparation

(1) Avoiding distraction, which counters concentration

(a) Distraction by the object

(i) Controlling the senses by transforming one's inner thoughts

I. Guarding the senses from others' wives

> Do not gaze on others' wives, but if you do,
> Regard them as your mother, child, or sib,
> Depending on their age. Should lust arise,
> Think well: they are by nature unclean filth. (21)

Do not gaze at other people's wives with designs, and **even if you do look at them, try and think of them, depending on their age, as your mother** if they are older, **as a daughter** if they are younger, **and as a sister** if they are the same age as you. And **if** that does not work and **you** still **feel lustful, reflect well on their unclean nature**, on their unpleasant smell and so on.

II. Guarding the senses from other desires

> Guard this fickle mind as you would do
> Your learning, children, treasure, or your life.
> Renounce all sensual pleasure as if it were
> A viper, poison, weapon, foe, or fire. (22)

If thinking in this way still does not stop you, you must guard your mind as follows. **Guard the mind, which moves** onto objects without staying still for a single second, from objects that tend to give rise constantly to afflictive emotions. How can one do this? Guard the mind **in the same way as** you protect **what you have learnt** from being forgotten;[25] guard the mind **like a** beloved **child**; guard it **as you would** some valuable **treasure**; guard the mind **as if it were your** cherished **life**. And that is not all. Concerning the pleasures of the senses, Nagarjuna instructs us to **shy away from** all **sensual pleasure as if it were a venomous** snake, a noxious **poison**, a lethal **weapon, an enemy** obstructing one's temporal life and happiness, **or a fire** burning one. As we find in a sutra:

Throughout, from very first to very last,
Virtue's like a mother, ever fair.
So why do childish beings abandon it
And lust for all the things that they desire?

III. The fault in not controlling the senses

The pleasures we desire will bring us ruin,
They're like the kimba fruit, the Buddha said.
Eschew them, it's their chains that tightly bind
The worldly in samsara's prison-house. (23)

You might say, "Don't pleasurable experiences give rise to happiness?" Although for ordinary people **pleasures** may appear to be related to happiness at the time they are enjoyed, in the end **they are their undoing. They are, the Sovereign of the Conquerors said, like the fruit of the kimba** tree, which grows in the western continent of Aparogodaniya: its skin is attractive but it is unpleasant inside; or it tastes delicious when one first eats it, but later it makes one ill. So, advises Nagarjuna, **give up these** pleasures, for it is **the chains**—the afflictive emotions—**of** attachment to pleasure that tightly **bind the worldly in the prison of samsara**.

IV. In praise of those who are able to control their senses

Of he whose fickle senses are controlled—
These six that never cease to dart at things—
And he who's fought and conquered many foes,
The first is truly brave, the wise have said. (24)

The six sense organs, the eyes and so forth, change **constantly** as they encounter **their objects**, form and the others: they are **unstable**, making the mind **flit** towards their objects. **Of the individual** who is able to use antidotes to control these six sense organs and **someone who is** courageous **in battle** and **victorious over** all the **hordes of enemies** one could possibly defeat, the bravest, **the real hero, the wise have said, is the first**, the winner in the battle with the senses. For while we see plenty of people who win wars, there are no ordinary beings who manage to conquer their senses.

(ii) Getting rid of attachment by recognizing the characteristics of the object

I. Getting rid of attachment by fully recognizing that the chief source of desire in the world of desire is the female body

Regard a young girl's body on its own,
Its smell so foul, its openings nine—a pot
Of filth, insatiable, and clothed with skin.
Regard too her adornments on their own. (25)

Earlier Nagarjuna referred to the unclean nature of women's bodies.[26] In what way are they to be regarded as impure? If you consider **a young woman's body on its own**, unadorned, it **smells unpleasant, has nine orifices** leaking foul matter, and is full of dirty things like excrement and urine. It **is like a jar containing all sorts of filth, difficult to fill**—for it is never satisfied, however much it has to eat and drink—**and covered with skin**, which is devoid of essence.[27] That is all there is to it.

You might argue that it is the things she adorns herself with that make one want her. But if you **look at her adornments too, on their own**, away from the body, you will no longer feel desire. As *The Way of the Bodhisattva* puts it:

The scent that now perfumes the skin
Is sandalwood and nothing else.
Yet how is it that one thing's fragrance
Causes you to long for something else?[28]

II. Getting rid of attachment by understanding the way desire generally functions

A man with leprosy, consumed by germs,
Will stand before the fire for comfort's sake
But still find no relief, so know the same is true
For those attached to the pleasures they desire. (26)

This verse shows the defect of attachment in the subject. In their longing to be **comfortable, lepers afflicted by the microbes** consuming them **stand close to a fire, but there still is no relief** for afterwards their distress again increases. **Know that the same is also true for** childish beings **who are attached to pleasures.** As *The Jewel Garland* says:

If bliss it is to scratch an itch,
What greater bliss no itch at all?
So too, the worldly, desirous, find some bliss,
But greatest is the bliss with no desire.

(b) Distraction by the eight ordinary concerns

(i) The antidote

I. The antidote itself

In order that you see the absolute,
Get used to truly understanding things.
No other practice is there such as this
Possessed of special virtues such as these. (27)

Because it is the domain of the highest wisdom, **the absolute truth**—the unmistaken thatness—has **to be seen** with the eye of primal wisdom, and **in order to** do this you must examine outer and inner **things,** such as form, with superior intelligence and thereby **reach a correct understanding** that they are devoid of true existence. **Get used to this** again and again. **There is no other method** in the world **that has the special qualities** of **this sort of** perfect intelligence that can overcome afflictive emotions and arouse primal wisdom, their antidote.

II. The advantages of having the antidote and disadvantages of not having it

To those possessed of breeding, learning, handsome looks,
Who have no wisdom, neither discipline, you need not bow.
But those who do have these two qualities,
Though lacking other virtues, you should revere. (28)

People who come from a good family, who are good-looking, and learned in all the sutras and shastras, **and yet do not have** the twin virtues of **wisdom** (the realization of the natural state) and **discipline** (whereby they avoid breaking their vows) possess none of the good qualities of the holy beings and **are** therefore **not** worthy of **reverence. On the other hand, those who possess these two virtues** of wisdom and discipline **are to be** respectfully **venerated even if they lack other qualities**, such as breeding and good looks, because anyone who has the wisdom to know what to do and what not to do, and the discipline to not indulge in negative actions, is to be counted as a holy being.

(ii) What to give up

I. The eight ordinary concerns that have to be given up

> You who know the world, take gain and loss,
> Or bliss and pain, or kind words and abuse,
> Or praise and blame—these eight mundane concerns—
> Make them the same, and don't disturb your mind. (29)

People meditating on emptiness in formal meditation sessions must not be carried away in the postmeditation period by the eight ordinary concerns. For this reason Nagarjuna addresses the king, "**You who** are thoroughly **knowledgeable** on the right **world**ly ways," and instructs him thus: "**Acquiring** wealth **and losing** it; **being happy** (having pleasurable experiences) **and unhappy** (experiencing suffering); hearing **pleasant** words and **unpleasant** ones; being **praised** openly and **criticized** behind one's back—these **are known as** the eight preoccupations common to ordinary worldly folk, with their different happy and unhappy moods. If you are to attain the state beyond the world, **equalize these eight worldly concerns without dwelling on them** as being things to be happy or sad about."

II. Advice on giving up the negative actions that result from these

A. The advice itself

> Perform no evil, even for the sake
> Of brahmins, bhikshus, gods, or honored guests,
> Your father, mother, queen, or for your court.
> The ripened fruit in hell's for you alone. (30)

One might wonder whether it is wrong to commit negative actions for the sake of one's teacher, or brahmins, and so on. O King, **you must not**

commit negative actions even for the sake of brahmins, monks, gods, guests, your **parents, queen, or court. The ripened result** of negative deeds, **hell,** is allotted to you alone, the person who has done them, and to no one else as accomplice: **no one** but you **will receive** your **allotted fate.**

B. Why it is necessary to avoid negative actions

Although performing wrong and evil deeds
Does not at once, like swords, create a gash,
When death arrives, those evil acts will show,
Their karmic fruit will clearly be revealed. (31)

Someone with nihilist views might say that the fully ripened effect of negative actions done in this life cannot be seen now, so it will not occur in the next life. But **even though the performance of evil deeds does not immediately cut one as** when one touches **a** sharp **weapon**—in other words, it does not make one suffer straightaway—**when the time comes to die, the result of the negative actions, whatever it may be**—being tortured by Yama's brutal henchmen and so on—**will become clearly evident,** as described in *The Way of the Bodhisattva*:

Your tear-stained cheeks, your red and swollen eyes,
Such will be the depths of your distress.
You'll gaze into the faces of your hopeless friends,
And see the coming servants of the Deadly Lord.

The memory of former sins will torture you,
The screams and din of hell break on your ears.
With very terror you will foul yourself,
What will you do then, in such extremity of fear?[29]

(c) Distraction by wealth

(i) A general explanation of the kinds of wealth to be adopted and abandoned

> Faith and ethics, learning, bounteousness,
> A flawless sense of shame and decency,
> And wisdom are the seven riches Buddha taught.
> Know, other common riches have no worth. (32)

The Capable One spoke of the following attributes as the **seven** noble **riches**, for they are the causes of untainted happiness and are not in any way ordinary. **Faith**—that is, the three kinds of faith[30] in the Three Jewels and confidence in the law of actions and their effects. **Discipline**, the avoidance of harmful actions. **Learning** that comes from listening to the holy Dharma that leads to liberation, with the intention of gaining complete knowledge. **Being generous**—with a desire to make offerings and to help beings, to give away all one's possessions without expecting anything in return or any karmic reward. **A sense of shame** with respect to oneself that prevents one from indulging in negative actions, and that is **unstained** by such things as jealousy or seeking veneration. **A sense of decency** with regard to others that stops one from engaging in unvirtuous practices. And **wisdom**, that is, knowledge of the particular and general characteristics of phenomena.[31]

You should realize that other common things that the world calls **riches**—gold, for instance—**are of no value** in obtaining untainted qualities; they are worthless, hollow, and without essence.

(ii) Specific trivial pursuits to be given up

> Gambling, public spectacles and shows,
> And indolence, bad company, strong drink,
> And nightly prowls—these six will lead to lower realms
> And damage your good name, so give them up. (33)

Playing dice and other **gambling games**, attending **public** spectacles, **idling around** with no inclination to do positive actions, **keeping the company of evil friends, drinking, prowling around at night** in order to steal—these six lead to rebirth **in the lower realms** in your next life, and in this life are causes for **your reputation being spoilt**. Therefore, Nagarjuna advises, **give up these six.**

(iii) The antidote to use for giving these up

I. The advantages of using the antidote

> Of all great wealth, contentment is supreme,
> Said he who taught and guided gods and men.
> So always be content; if you know this
> Yet have no wealth, true riches you'll have found. (34)

Of all the valuable things there are, like gold and silver, **the very greatest** of riches is **to be content** and have little desire for such things, **as the Teacher of gods and men,** the Buddha Bhagavan, **has declared** in the *Sutra Requested by Surata*:

> *For those who stay forever generous*
> *Although they've not a single bite to eat,*
> *The greatest wealth on earth is truly theirs,*
> *'Tis thus explained by those with perfect sight.*

Therefore, **in all circumstances be content. When you know contentment, even if you do not possess** a little gold or other **valuable things, you will be truly rich,** because once content, you have achieved the very reason for acquiring things.[32]

II. The disadvantages of not having that antidote

> Kind Sir, to own a lot brings so much misery,
> There's no such grief for those with few desires.
> The more the naga lords possess of heads,
> The more their headaches, the more they have of cares. (35)

"**Kind Sir,**" says Nagarjuna, addressing the king (for he is someone who is easy to get along with), **inasmuch as those who have a lot of things** like gold and other possessions **must suffer,** first in acquiring them, then in guarding them, and finally in seeing them dispersed, **those with few desires have no such** suffering. To take an example, the **more** snake **heads the supreme nagas** (the naga kings) have, **the more headaches** they are liable to get. Some commentaries explain this metaphor as follows: the more heads the naga kings have, each head bearing a crown jewel, the greater the misery the naga kings experience guarding those jewels.

(d) Distraction by pleasurable indulgence

(i) Giving up attachment to one's spouse

I. Spouses to be avoided

> A murderess who sides with enemies,
> A queen who holds her husband in contempt,
> A thieving wife who steals the smallest thing—
> It's these three kinds of wife you must avoid. (36)

There are three kinds of wife you should avoid. One who **naturally sides with one's enemies** and goes around with other men, and who out of jealousy wants to kill her husband, **like a murderer**. One who does not honor her **husband**, but treats him **contemptuously, like a queen**. And one who **steals the smallest thing**, not to speak of valuables, **like a thief**.

II. Those to be taken as a wife

> A wife who like a sister follows you,
> Affectionate like a true and loving friend,
> Supportive like a mother, obedient like a maid—
> She must be honored like a family god. (37)

You might wonder, then, what kind of person you should marry. A wife who is **like a sister emulating** her brother: she follows her husband without scorning what he says. A wife who is **like a close friend** with whom one gets on very well and who takes care of one: she is a **true friend.** A wife who is **like a mother** wanting to help her child: her **desire is to help** her husband. **And** a wife **who is like a maid** obeying when one makes her happy: she **submits to** one's **authority. Such** wives will not dishonor one's family and so **are to be** relied upon or **honored like a family god**.

(ii) Giving up attachment to food

> Take food as medicine, in the right amount,
> Without attachment, without hatefulness:
> Don't eat for vanity, for pride or ego's sake,
> Eat only for your body's sustenance. (38)

When you eat **food, it should be** in the right amount, **like medicine** that does the body good. In doing so, **use food without** an attitude of **attachment** or **hatred**, reflected in the way you eat: **do not** eat **because of vanity**, wanting to be tough, **nor because of** hatred, **arrogantly** thinking, "I will build up my physical strength and beat up my enemies," **nor** in order to strengthen your various limbs or **in order to take care of** your body, to take care of "me." Eat **simply to sustain your body** as a means for accomplishing positive actions.

(iii) Giving up attachment to sleep

> O Knowledgeable One, recite all day
> And in the first and last watch of the night.
> Then in between these two sleep mindfully
> So that your slumbers are not spent in vain. (39)

Great being, you who know what to do and what not to do, **having** spent **the whole of the day and the first and last** of the three **watches of the night reciting**, meditating, and so on, in the middle of the night **too, while you are asleep, do not let your slumber be fruitless** or pointless but **keep mindful**, thinking that you will rise quickly and put your efforts into practicing virtue. In this manner, **sleep in between these** first and last watches: as a result of your attitude, your sleep will become positive.

(2) Practicing the four boundless qualities as an aid to concentration

> Constantly and perfectly reflect
> On love, compassion, joy, impartiality.
> And should you not attain the higher state,
> At least you will find bliss in Brahma's world. (40)

Focusing on all sentient beings, practice the four boundless qualities: **love**, which is the wish that they be happy; **compassion**, the wish that they be free from suffering; **sympathetic joy**, which is to feel happy when they are happy; and **impartiality**, which is to treat them impartially as equals, without attachment or aversion.

Of these four, the meaning of the term "boundless love" is that one focuses on boundless sentient beings (as the object of concentration) and that boundless merit comes to the meditator.

For compassion and the others there are three categories: compassion focusing on sentient beings; focusing on phenomena; and without concepts. The first is that of ordinary beings and takes the form of wishing that all may be free from suffering. The second, focusing on phenomena, is that of sublime beings of the Shravaka and Pratyekabuddha vehicles who, since they have realized the no-self of the individual, designate merely the phenomena of the aggregates as sentient beings;[33] it takes the form of the wish that they may themselves be free from suffering. The third, being without concepts, takes the form of viewing sentient beings as illusion-like through realizing the no-self of phenomena, and wishing they be free from suffering. This is the compassion that the sublime beings of the Great Vehicle have.

According to *The Ornament of the Mahayana Sutras*, the Shravakas and Pratyekabuddhas do have realization of the no-self of phenomena, in which case the last two categories belong to all the sublime beings of the three vehicles. They have one essence but different aspects.

How should one meditate on these four boundless qualities? Divide beings into three categories: friends, enemies, and those that are neither. Begin by concentrating on your parents, relatives, and friends, and meditate by wishing that they may meet with happiness and so forth. After that do the same focusing on beings who are neither your friends nor your enemies. Finally, meditate focusing on all those for whom you feel enmity. The meditation is said to be perfect and complete when one's enemies and one's relatives and friends become the same.

As for the scope of the meditation, concentrate first on the beings in Jambudvipa, then on those in the universe of a billion worlds, and then on all the beings filling the whole of space.

Meditate constantly and well on these four boundless qualities and through the wisdom of these boundless qualities you will attain nirvana.

Even if you **do not attain the higher** state of nirvana immediately, **you will gain the happiness of the** first **Brahma world.**[34]

ii. The actual practice, meditating on the four concentrations[35]

> The four samadhis, which in turn discard
> Pursuit of pleasure, joy and bliss and pain,
> Will lead to fortune equal to the gods'
> In Brahma, Light, Great Virtue, or Great Fruit. (41)

The first concentration comprises the antidote branch—discursive thinking and subtle analysis—used to abandon **the pursuit of pleasure**, that is to say, yearning for pleasure and wanting to get rid of anything that irritates one; the joy and bliss that arise from solitude; and the one-pointed concentration characterized by the latter.

The second concentration comprises the antidote branch—a very clear mind—used to abandon analysis; the **joy and** bliss that come from concentration;[36] and the one-pointed concentration characterized by the latter.

The third concentration comprises the antidote branch—mindfulness, vigilance, and evenness—used to abandon joy; **bliss; and** the one-pointed concentration characterized by the latter.

The fourth concentration comprises the antidote branch—perfect mindfulness and evenness—used to **completely eliminate** bliss and **sufferings;** neutrality of feeling; and the one-pointed concentration characterized by the latter.

By meditating on these **four** causal **concentrations**, Nagarjuna says, **one attains the same fortunate** rebirths **as the gods of** the four resultant concentrations, which are subdivided into lesser, middling, and greater categories as follows. The realm of the first concentration consists of **The Pure**, Priests of Brahma and Great Pure Ones;[37] the realm of the second concentration likewise comprises Dim Light, Measureless Light, and **Clear Light**; that of the third concentration is divided into Lesser Virtue, Limitless Virtue, **and Flourishing Virtue; and** the realm of the fourth concentration consists of Cloudless, Merit-Born, and **Great Result**.

iii. The postmeditation

(1) Positive and negative actions that have to be adopted or given up generally

(a) The relative gravity of positive and negative actions

> Great good and evil deeds are of five kinds,
> Determined by their constancy, their zeal,
> Their lack of counteragent, their perfect fields.
> So strive in this respect to practice good. (42)

There are **five great kinds of positive or negative actions**. (1) **Actions** that are performed **constantly** (with a constant underlying attitude) and that are special in terms of their application. (2) Those that are done with **great determination** (as the attitude of the moment) and that are special in terms of their intention. (3) Those that have **nothing to counter them**, that is, an opposing action that can destroy them, and are special in terms of counteragent. And beneficial or harmful acts that are special in terms of their field, this being of two kinds: (4) "beneficial fields" such as parents and teachers and in particular bears, monkeys, and so forth that have helped one as in the stories of the Buddha's previous lives; and (5) "**fields who have the most essential qualities**," that is, the Three Jewels and those who have risen out of the samadhi of cessation.

Make an effort, therefore, to avoid great negative actions and to **practice** great **positive actions**.

(b) Cultivating powerful positive actions as antidotes to negative acts

> A pinch of salt can give its salty taste
> To a little water, but not to the Ganges stream.
> So know that, likewise, minor evil deeds
> Can never change a mighty source of good. (43)

Just as a little salt—a few fractions of a measure—can make a small amount of water taste salty but **cannot** change a huge **river like the Ganges, know that in the same way even a small negative action** can harm someone whose positive deeds are weak but cannot harm anyone who has frequently performed **an immensely positive action**, vast in scope. Here,

Nagarjuna is instructing us to apply ourselves to powerful positive actions repeatedly on a vast scale.

(2) How to avoid the things that hinder concentration in particular

> Wildness and remorse, and hateful thoughts,
> And dullness-somnolence, and yearning lust,
> And doubt are hindrances—please know these five
> Are thieves that steal the gem of virtuous deeds. (44)

There now follows an explanation of how the five "hindrances" are the enemies of the samadhis, perfect freedoms, and so forth,[38] and must therefore be assiduously avoided.

Wildness, where the mind proceeds out towards objects that attract it, **and remorse**, where one thinks of evil acts one has done. These come under the same sphere as movement and so their antidote is sustained calm. They are nourished by four things: thinking about one's relatives, thinking about one's country, thinking that one will not die, and remembering the games, laughs, and good times one enjoyed in the past. Since wildness and remorse are both nourished by the same things, they are counted as a single hindrance.

Malice, which is the agitation in the mind caused by things that arouse hatred. In the explanation that follows on how discipline is hindered, it is grouped with craving (see below), but in the context of the five hindrances such hatred is counted as a single hindrance. Its antidote is patience.

Dullness, in which body and mind are disinclined to meditate and one feels in low spirits, and **somnolence**, where the mind, powerless, withdraws and folds in on itself. These come under the same sphere as dull-wittedness and lack of clarity and are therefore counted as one. Their antidote is clarity. They are nourished by five things: feeling thick—unclear, heavy, and disconnected; unhappiness; stretching; indigestion; and feeling low-spirited.

An inclination—through craving—**for** the five **pleasures** of the senses such as food and sex. This is counted as one in the context of the five hindrances, though as a hindrance to discipline it is taught as being classed with malice (see above). Its antidote is to meditate on ugliness and give up attachment.

Indecision, where one is of two minds concerning liberation and the path to liberation.

Know that these five hindrances are thieves that rob you of the jewel of virtue, and avoid them, advises Nagarjuna.

Craving and hatred both adversely affect the superior training in discipline. The reasons for this are, respectively, that when one is influenced by craving for pleasure one will not take up discipline properly in the first place; and that once one has taken it up, when other people admonish one to follow the precepts correctly, one gets angry and cannot accomplish anything properly in accord with the Dharma.

Dullness and somnolence both impair superior concentration because when one meditates on the causes of sustained calm—the four boundless qualities and so forth—they make the mind low-spirited.

Wildness and remorse adversely affect superior wisdom because when one meditates on the reasons for concentrating they cause the mind to be distracted.

Indecision adversely affects both one-pointedness and wisdom because when one meditates on the causes of the equanimity that is the union of sustained calm and profound insight, as a result of doubt one cannot reach a decision and one is unable to settle in equanimity.

Since they obscure the samadhis and perfect freedoms and so forth, or the three precious trainings, it has been said, "Be diligent in avoiding the five hindrances."

f. Wisdom

i. A brief account of the essence of the path with the five elements beginning with confidence[39]

(1) What one has to adopt: confidence and the other elements

> With faith and diligence and mindfulness,
> And concentration, wisdom, five in all,
> You must strive hard to reach the "highest state":
> As "powers" these "forces" take you to the "peak." (45)

Five elements are described in this verse. **Confidence**, namely confidence in the Four Noble Truths; **diligence**, that is to say, genuine joy in adoption and rejection related to the Four Noble Truths; **mindfulness**—never letting the objects to be meditated on slip one's mind; **concentration**, that is to say, one-pointed focus supported by mindfulness of the four truths; and **wisdom**, which perfectly discerns them when one settles evenly in concentration. At the time these five become the direct cause leading to the sublime path we speak of the **supreme mundane level**.[40] At the stage of "acceptance" they are referred to as the **five** irresistible forces, for they cannot be overcome by adverse factors. **Apply yourself assiduously to these** and get used to them. **They** are first referred to here as **irresistible forces** for the stage of "acceptance," but at the stage of "warmth" they are known as "**powers**" because they make one more powerful for clearly seeing the truth. As these powers increase **one reaches the "peak,"** because one's sources of good become unwavering. This verse, therefore, is an instruction on being diligent.[41]

(2) What one has to abandon: how to get rid of arrogance by means of an antidote

> "I'm not beyond my karma, the deeds I've done;
> I'll still fall ill, age, die, and leave my friends."
> Think like this again and yet again
> And with this remedy avoid all arrogance. (46)

"I will be **sick**, I will **grow old**, I will **die**, I will be **separated from those I love**, my relations and so forth. **In such manner**, the fully ripened effect of my **actions** will come to me and to no one else, and I am therefore **not**

above depending on **what I did** in former lives." **To think like this again and again is the antidote** to such things as arrogance: make every effort **not to become arrogant** by meditating on this antidote.

ii. Detailed explanation of wisdom: close mindfulness and the other elements[42]

(1) Showing that wisdom is the root of all happiness in samsara and nirvana

(a) The right view of worldly people, which is the root of both higher rebirth and lasting happiness

> If higher birth and freedom is your quest,
> You must become accustomed to right views.
> Those who practice good with inverse views
> Will yet experience terrible results. (47)

Nagarjuna begins with the following exhortation: **If you truly seek the higher realms** (the abodes of gods and men) and **liberation** (that is to say, the levels and paths leading to omniscience), you must constantly **get used to the right view**; for confidence in the law of karma, with the relative view concerning subject and object, is the cause of higher rebirth, while the wisdom that realizes the true nature of subject and object is the cause of liberation.

What fault, you might ask, would there be in not having the right view? **People who have wrong views** with regard to actions, cause and effect, completely destroy their sources of good. At the same time, **however many positive deeds they may perform**, such as acts of generosity, those who are very attached to material things, and who do not have the view or realization that they are empty, possess the **terrible** cause of rebirth in samsara as the **fully ripened effect of all their actions**.

(b) The right supramundane view that leads to lasting happiness

> Know this truth: that men are ever sad,
> Impermanent, devoid of self, impure.
> Those who do not have close mindfulness,
> Their view four times inverted, head for ruin. (48)

Looking at things with the three kinds of wisdom,[43] **know that human beings are in truth unhappy** on account of the three types of suffering;[44] they are **impermanent** with each instant that passes; **devoid of self**, since there is no doer; and, as regards their flesh, bones, blood, and so forth, **impure. Those who are not closely mindful** of these four and who do not examine them with wisdom **view things in four mistaken ways:** they see their impure bodies as pure, the suffering they experience as happiness, the impermanent mind as permanent, and selfless phenomena as a self. Such people **are destroyed** by the suffering of samsara and the lower realms, so for this reason you must be diligent in closely applying mindfulness.

(2) The main explanation: the path endowed with such wisdom

(a) Specific explanations

(i) Ascertaining the no-self of the individual

> Form is not the self, the Buddha taught,
> And self does not have form, nor dwell in form,
> While form dwells not in self. Thus you must see
> The four remaining aggregates are empty too. (49)

If there is a single self, is its nature that of the aggregates—form and the rest? Or does it exist as something else? The answer to the first question is "No." The scriptural authority for this is a sutra, which states, "Form is not the self ...," and continues until, "... consciousness is not the self."[45] Reasoning also applies, as follows. **Form is not the self**; if the self were the same as form and the other aggregates, it would have to be impermanent and multiple. And if you assert that form and the other aggregates exist substantially, then the self must exist substantially and the clinging to an "I" would be the subject of a substantial thing, in which case you would be viewing things correctly and it would therefore be impossible to use an antidote to get rid of the seed.[46]

This is affirmed in *Introduction to the Middle Way*:

> *But if the self were equal to the aggregates,*
> *It must, since these are many, be a multiplicity.*
> *The self would be substantial, and seeing it as such*
> *Would not at all be incorrect.*[47]

One might ask, are form and the rest something else? Does the self use form and the other aggregates as a support in the same way that Devadatta—that is, any person—makes use of his wealth, cattle, bed, trees, and so forth? In the first place, this is not the case, for the scriptures say, "**The self does not possess form** ..." and so on to, "... it does not possess consciousness." And reasoning shows that, unlike Devadatta who has control over his cattle, the self does not possess form and so on as things to be controlled, because we can see that form and the other aggregates, without the self wanting it, change into something else and perish.

Aggregates that are different from the self are also not possible from a second point of view. Form and the rest are not multiple locations for the self to dwell in, as the scriptures show: "**The self does not dwell in form** ..." and so on to, "... the self does not dwell in consciousness." And reason tells us that, unlike Devadatta sitting on a woven mat, the self cannot dwell in form and the other aggregates as though using them as a support; for if that were the case, the aggregates being impermanent, it would follow that the self, too, would be impermanent.

There is yet a third point of view, stated in the scriptures as follows: "**Form does not dwell in the self** ..." and so on to, "... consciousness does not dwell in the self." The reasoning is that the aggregates do not dwell in the self, supported by it in the same way that a tree is supported by the earth, because aggregates taking the support of a permanent self could never perish. Furthermore, their birth and destruction would depend on the self and this does not happen because one conceives of the creation and destruction of outer forms as occurring without a self.

This is how we investigate form. **In the same way, you should also realize** profound **emptiness**, as it is, in **the four remaining aggregates** (feeling and so forth), using scriptural authority and reason, as explained above, to show that there is no self that is of the same nature as the aggregates or different from them.

Explaining things the other way round, it is said in the sutras that for each of the five aggregates there are four views—the view of form as the self, and so on—making twenty extreme views in all. The Buddha taught that the antidote to these is "Form is not the self."

(ii) Investigating the aggregates that are the support of the self

> The aggregates are not a simple whim,
> From neither time nor nature do they come,
> Nor by themselves, from God, or without cause;
> Their source, you ought to know, is ignorance,
> From karmic deeds and craving have they come. (50)

Form and the other aggregates do not happen adventitiously, merely out of wishful thinking, with no dependence on other conditions: **the aggregates are not a result of one's own fanciful thinking**, because they arise from individual causes and conditions. **Neither** do they arise **from** something eternal in **time**, as the Eternalists would claim, since there is no time that is independent of causes and conditions. Since a result cannot be produced from a permanent entity, they do **not** happen **from** transformation by a single permanent **nature**, the *prakriti* ("primal substance"), in which *rajas, tamas,* and *sattva* are in equilibrium, as the Samkhyas claim. And since a fruit cannot be produced from a seed without the seed being altered and without depending on conditions, they do **not** happen **by themselves**, as the Mimamsakas hold. They do **not** come **from** the Naiyayika School's **Ishvara,**[48] because a result comes from a cause that has to precede it. **Neither** do they come into being **without a cause**: if they arose without a cause, they would either have had to have been there all the time or never ever be![49]

Then what cause do they come from? To take an example, just as a shoot is produced by watering a healthy seed covered with manure, **know that** the aggregates **come from** powerful karmic **actions** covered by **unknowing**—that is to say, ignorance—**and**, as it were, moistened by **craving**.

(b) The actual path

(i) The three fetters, which are incompatible with the path

> To feel that one is ethically superior,
> To view one's body wrongly, and to doubt—
> With these three fetters, you should understand,
> The way through freedom's city gates is blocked. (51)

Ethical **superiority**, which is to consider that **discipline** and **ascetic practices** based on wrong views purify or lead to liberation; **the view** of the transitory composite, whereby one **mistakenly** regards **one's body**, the five causal aggregates, as "I" and "mine"; and **doubt**, where one is of two minds about liberation and the path of liberation, are **fetters that bind one.**[50] Because of the view of the transitory composite, one has no wish to proceed to liberation. Because of superiority one mistakes the path. And because of doubt one meets with hindrances. **Know that these three close the gates of the city of liberation**, and rid yourself of them. As we read in a sutra:

No wish to leave, losing the way,
And torn by doubts as to the path—
The way to freedom is thus blocked.

(ii) Diligence, which is a favorable condition

Freedom will depend on you alone
And there is no one else, no friend can help.
So bring endeavor to the Four Noble Truths
With study, discipline, and concentration. (52)

What we call **liberation** is nothing other than the mind being free from the bonds of afflictive emotions. It **depends on** training by **oneself** on the path of liberation. **For that, there is no** question of **being assisted by someone else**; you have to endeavor on your own.
How can one attain liberation? It is said:

By observing discipline, hearing, and reflecting
Apply yourself to meditation.

This means **listening** many times to the Buddha's teachings relating to the Four Noble Truths **and**, with determination to be free, observing whichever **discipline** you can of the seven kinds of pratimoksha vows—those of the bhikshu or bhikshuni, male or female shramanera, male or female upasaka, and woman novice. **By means of** the one-pointed concentration of the four **concentrations**[51]—The Pure, Great Pure Ones, and so forth—direct your attention to the **Four Noble Truths**—the truth of suffering and the rest—and meditate on their true nature: in relative truth, their sixteen subdivisions beginning with impermanence; and in absolute truth, emptiness free from all conceptual extremes. **Be diligent** in knowing these crucial points of what to adopt and what to reject.

(iii) The three trainings, the essence of the path

I. A general exposition of the three trainings

> Train always in superior discipline,
> Superior wisdom, and superior mind.
> Monks' vows exceed a hundred and five tens,
> Yet they are all included in these three. (53)

The three trainings are: **superior discipline**, which is essentially the avoidance—dedicated entirely to going beyond suffering—of the seven negative actions;[52] **superior wisdom**, which is the realization of the two kinds of no-self; **and superior concentration**,[53] which essentially comprises the four concentrations consistent with and leading to the sublime path. Because they constitute a complete and unerring method for attaining liberation, you should **constantly train in them**. They are called "superior" because their purpose is to take one beyond suffering. Since the **more than** two **hundred and fifty precepts**, that is, the two hundred and fifty-three vows of a bhikshu taught in the pratimoksha—the four radical defeats, the thirteen residual faults, the thirty downfalls requiring rejection, the ninety "mere downfalls," the four faults to be specifically confessed, and the one hundred and twelve wrong actions—come under discipline, they **are fully included in the three** trainings. So make an effort to train in these.

II. A specific explanation of the training in wisdom

A. How to extract oneself from affliction[54]

1. How to turn the mind away from the things of this life

a. Brief introduction

> My lord, the Buddha taught close mindfulness
> Of body as the single path to tread.
> Hold fast and guard it well, for all the Dharma
> Is destroyed by loss of mindfulness. (54)

Mighty Lord, says Nagarjuna addressing the king, in all circumstances, whatever you are doing—standing up, sitting down, and so on—strictly maintain perfect **mindfulness** of phenomena **including the body** and so forth.[55] This, **the Sugata has shown**, is **the one way to proceed, the** certain **path** for easily attaining liberation, for it is written in a sutra:

> *O Monks, the path that purifies sentient beings, that takes them completely beyond suffering and happiness, that makes them understand the correct way, and makes nirvana manifest is this view—close attention to the body.*

Therefore, because this mindfulness of the body and so on is extremely important, **hold fast and guard it well**. Otherwise, **if** you fail to do so and **mindfulness is diminished, all virtuous practice will** also **be destroyed**, not to mention any chance of attaining nirvana.

b. Detailed explanation

i. Reflecting on the impermanence of life

(1) Meditating on impermanence by reflecting on the unpredictability of the time of death

> With all its many risks, this life endures
> No more than windblown bubbles in a stream.
> How marvellous to breathe in and out again,
> To fall asleep and then awake refreshed. (55)

An individual's **life** is subject to **many** kinds of **harm**, from humans and nonhumans externally and from illness and other disorders of the elements internally. It is **less enduring than a bubble in a stream blown about by the wind. What a wonder it is that one can breathe in** and then **breathe out** again, **fall asleep and wake up** again **refreshed** and still alive. As it is said:

> *Impermanent are the three worlds, like autumn clouds;*
> *Watch how beings live and die, it's but a dance;*
> *A person's life is as a flash of lightning in the sky,*
> *Like a mountain torrent it rushes swiftly on.*

(2) Meditating on impermanence by reflecting on the inevitability of death

> This body ends as ash, dry dust, or slime,
> And ultimately shit, no essence left.
> Consumed, evaporated, rotted down—
> Thus know its nature: to disintegrate. (56)

When its time is over, **the body ends up** being reduced to **ashes** by fire, being **dried up** by the sun and wind, or **decomposing** after being thrown into the river; eaten by animals it **finally** becomes **excrement**. So **know that** this body **has no essence**. **It will be consumed** by fire, it will be **reduced to nothing** by the sun and wind, broken down and **rotted away** by water; chopped into pieces as mouthfuls for animals, its very **nature** is to be **divided up**.

(3) Meditating on impermanence by reflecting on other aspects

> The ground, Mount Meru, and the oceans too
> Will be consumed by seven blazing suns;
> Of things with form no ashes will be left,
> No need to speak of puny, frail man. (57)

It is said that the mandala of the solid, firm material **ground, and Mount Meru** together with the seven golden mountain ranges, and even the outer and inner **oceans** will be destroyed by a universal fire. When this happens the first **sun** will burn up the trees and forests; the second sun will dry up the brooks; the third will dry up Lake Manasarowar and the four great rivers; the fourth and fifth will reduce the oceans to dew drops. The sixth will dry up everything, leaving not a drop of water. The great earth and Mount Meru will all go up in smoke. As the **seven**th sun rises everything will become a single tongue of fire, and not even ashes will be left. So **if**, after the seven suns have appeared, everything is **consumed by the blaze** in a single flame, so that **even these physical things**—these solid forms—are destroyed and **nothing, not even ash, is left, what need is there to mention the utterly frail human** body? It could not possibly last forever.

(4) A summary of the above

> It's all impermanent, devoid of self,
> So if you're not to stay there refugeless
> And helpless, drag your mind away, O King,
> From plantainlike samsara, which has no core. (58)

Thus, not only are all things that have form impermanent but so also, as explained above, are **all these** five causal aggregates **impermanent, devoid of self. There is no refuge** to protect you from suffering, **no helper** to support you, so if you are not to remain in this situation, **O Greatest of men** (meaning "King"), **you must**, with a sense of disenchantment, **drag your mind away from** this **circle of existence**, which is **without essence,** like a **plantain tree**.

ii. Reflecting on the difficulty of finding the freedoms and advantages

(1) How rare it is in general simply to be born as a human

(a) The rarity of a human birth

> Harder, harder still than that a turtle chance upon
> The opening in a yoke upon a great and single sea
> Is rebirth as a human after rebirth as a beast;
> So heed the sacred Dharma, King, and make your life bear fruit. (59)

If the world's great **oceans** were to become **one**, and in that ocean there lived a turtle that rose to the surface once in every hundred years; and if, on the surface, there were a **yoke** with a single opening, blown in all directions by the wind, **the turtle** might just, by **coincidence,** put its neck through **the opening** in the yoke. But it is **even harder** for a dumb **animal**, unable to give rise to any powerful positive actions, to migrate from the support of an animal body and **obtain** rebirth in **the human state**. For this reason, **Lord of men**, now that you have obtained the precious freedoms and advantages, **make** your human body **fruitful by** making the best use of it and **practicing the sacred Dharma**.

(b) Showing how despicable it is to practice negative actions with such a body

More stupid yet than one who throws some slops
Into a golden vessel all bejewelled
Is he who's gained a precious human birth
And wastes it in an evil, sinful life. (60)

Someone who were to sweep sewage—excrement, urine, and the like—**into a vessel** made of **gold** and **ornamented** with all kinds of **jewels** would be regarded with universal contempt, but **how much more dim-witted it is to do negative actions after being born as a human.** Not only is the human state harder to come by than golden vessels, but negative actions are much worse than sewage because they give rise to inexhaustible fully ripened effects. For this reason, once you have obtained this support for practicing positive actions, this human body, which is so difficult to come by, you must be diligent.

(2) Showing in particular the support endowed with the four wheels

(a) A general account of the four wheels as favorable conditions

To dwell in places that befit the task,
To follow and rely on holy beings,
Aspiring high, with merit from the past—
These four great wheels are yours for you to use. (61)

Regarding where you should live, **stay in a place that is compatible** with giving rise to the sublime path that increases virtue. As for whom to befriend and rely on, **follow a supreme being** who will make your faults diminish and good qualities grow. **Wish the best for yourself** in accomplishing enlightenment, so that by acting in accordance with your wishes you accomplish things properly. From having **created merit in previous lives** your mind will be completely mature.

These conditions are called "wheels" because they are like the wheels of a chariot. Just as a chariot with balanced wheels can swiftly reach its destination, so too with these conditions on the path, one can swiftly reach liberation. **You have the four great wheels**, and all the various causes for accomplishing the path are therefore complete, so be diligent in accomplishing the path.[56]

(b) A specific explanation of the spiritual friend

> The virtuous friend in whom to place your trust
> Has brought pure conduct to perfection, said the Lord.
> So follow holy beings, many are they
> Who relied upon the Buddhas and found peace. (62)

Someone who is accomplishing the path has first to **rely on a spiritual friend**. The latter has **perfected pure conduct** and is the cause that takes one beyond suffering, as **the Capable One declared**: "Ananda, thus it is: spiritual friends and virtuous companions are those who have brought pure conduct to perfection. As a result of this, Ananda, all those whose nature is to be born will be liberated from birth by relying on a spiritual friend ...." **For this reason**, constantly **follow holy beings. By relying on the Victorious Ones a very great many** sentient beings **have attained peace**. What then are the characteristics of a holy being? *The Ornament of the Mahayana Sutras* lists them as follows:

> *Take as a teacher someone peaceful, disciplined, perfectly peaceful,*
> *Possessed of superior qualities, endeavor, and knowledge of*
> *the texts,*[57]
> *Who understands them fully, and is skilled at explaining them,*
> *Is full of love, and never tires of teaching.*

In other words, he observes the three precious trainings,[58] he is richly endowed with the transmissions of the Three Pitakas, he has realized the absolute nature as it is, he is skilled in teaching others and explaining the words, he is loving towards disciples and others, and he never tires of teaching by giving instructions and advice.

(3) Reflecting on how to be free of the eight unfavorable conditions of lack of opportunity

To be reborn with false beliefs, or yet
As animals, or pretas, or in hell,
Deprived of Buddha's words, barbarians
In border lands, or reborn dull and dumb, (63)

Or born among the long-lived gods—
Of these eight defective states that give no opportunity
You must be free, and, finding opportunity,
Be diligent, to put a stop to birth. (64)

The following kinds of rebirth **are known as the eight defective states of lack of opportunity.** To be born **holding wrong views** and scorning the law of cause and effect. To be **born as an animal, as a preta, or in the hells** (thus making three unfavorable states in the lower realms). To be born **bereft of the Conqueror's teachings**, that is, born in a world where no Buddhas have appeared, **or** even if they have appeared, to be **born as a barbarian in a border country** where one does not even hear the word "Buddha"; **or** even if born in a central land,[59] to be born **dull and dumb**, in the sense of being mentally defective and unable to speak (making four in the human realm).[60] Or to be **born as a long-lived god** lacking the perception of being sentient (making one in the gods' realm).[61] **Once one has found** the extraordinary human body that is **free of these** eight defects **and provides the opportunity** to accomplish the path of liberation, one must make it meaningful; so, advises Nagarjuna, **work hard** to accomplish the path properly **in order to stop rebirth** in samsara.

2. How to turn the mind away from the whole of samsara: reflecting on the defects of samsara

a. Brief introduction

O Gentle Sir, to make your disenchantment grow
With this samsara, source of many pains—
Desires frustrated, death, ill health, old age—
Please heed its defects, even just a few. (65)

Gentle Sir, says Nagarjuna, addressing the king, since samsara is **the source of many kinds of suffering—frustrated desires** for food, clothes, and so forth, **and** finally **death**, with, in the meantime, **illness** as the elements change, **ageing** as one's youth transforms, and misery, lamentation, **and so on—it is samsara that you must weary of.** If you do not drag your mind away from samsara, you will never think of striving for liberation. And since just talking about **a few** of **its**—samsara's—**defects** helps to do that, I will mention them briefly in order to inspire weariness in you, so **please listen.**

b. Detailed explanation

i. How nothing can be relied on even if it looks like happiness

(1) How nothing can be relied on

(a) How, since one cannot be certain who is a friend and who an enemy, it is inappropriate to rely on anyone

> Men who've fathered sons in turn are sons,
> And mothers likewise daughters. Bitter foes
> Turn into friends, the converse too is true.
> Because of this samsara's never sure. (66)

In taking birth again and again, **fathers** sometimes become **sons, mothers** become **daughters,** and even **people who have been enemies** become **close friends** in other lives. And **vice versa**: sons become fathers and so on. **Because of this there is no certainty at all that in samsara** one ends up as one thing, either friend or enemy. So get rid of attachment and aversion, taking sides with friends and against enemies.

(b) How one can never be satisfied

> Know that every being has drunk more milk
> Than all the four great oceans could contain,
> And still, by emulating common folk,
> They'll circle, drinking ever more and more. (67)

Know that every sentient being **has drunk more milk** in the past **than** could be contained in **the four** great **oceans** in the four directions, there being no number to their births on the earth. And **even now, as samsaric beings who** have not set out on the sublime path and **are following the path of ordinary**, samsaric **individuals, they will drink** milk **in even greater quantities** than before, because for childish beings who have not cultivated positive actions consistent with liberation there is no end to their circling in samsara.

(c) How it is impossible to predict when it will all end

> A heap of all the bones each being has left
> Would reach to Meru's top or even higher.
> To count one's mother's lineage with pills
> The size of berries, the earth would not suffice. (68)

The **pile of** the **bones each being** has had in previous lives **is as big as Mount Meru** or **even surpasses it in height**, and still more bones, many more than that, will have to be left behind if one does not make efforts on the path.

Even if one tried to count all one's maternal ancestors by fashioning **pills the size of juniper berries** from the earth of this planet and counting them, one would run out of **earth without ever reaching** the end. A single being could never finish counting the number of mothers he has had, so how many myriads more will there be to come if one does not endeavor properly on the path? This has been explained in a sutra, where the Buddha says:

> *O monks, let us take an example. If someone were to make pilules the size of juniper berries from the Earth, putting each one aside and saying, "This one is my mother, that one is my mother's mother ...," and so on, I tell you, monks, before very long the mud from the Earth would run out, but not so the ancestral line of people's mothers.*

(d) How one's position is uncertain and cannot be relied on

(i) How great dominion cannot be relied on

> Indra, universally revered,
> Will fall again to earth through action's force.
> And he who ruled the universe as king
> Will be a slave within samsara's wheel. (69)

Having become Indra, worthy of the offerings of the world, for he is venerated by worldly gods not to mention everyone else, one will, **because of** the residual effect of one's **actions, again fall back onto the earth** among ordinary men or into the lower realms.

Even if one has become a universal monarch, possessing the seven precious attributes of royalty and having dominion over the four continents, when there is nothing left of one's past good deeds **one will,** on account of one's actions **in samsara, again** be reborn **into slavery** among men or fall into the lower realms.

(ii) How delightful company cannot be relied on

> For ages it was rapture to caress
> The lovely breasts and waists of heaven's maids,
> Now one will bear the terrible caress—
> The crush, the slash, and tear—of hell's machine. (70)

After being born as a god and **spending ages enjoying the pleasures of caressing the breasts and waists of maidens in the higher realms,** one has no good deeds left and as a result of one's negative actions one is **again** reborn **in the hells.** There, in the Crushing Hell, **one is crushed** between massive mountains of iron; in the Black Line Hell one is **carved up** with swords and other weapons; and in the Hells of Heat and Intense Heat **one is pierced and cut** with blazing pikes and with saws and so forth, and **pecked** and **clawed** by savage beasts. **Know** that for a very long time one will **endure the agonizing** pain that comes from **contact with the machinery** of hell.

(iii) How there is no essence to pleasant places

For years you might have stayed on Meru's crest
Delighting as it yielded underfoot,
But think now of the torment that will strike:
To wade through glowing coals and rotten flesh. (71)

After staying for a long time—thousands of god-years—**on the summit of Mount Meru**, which is made from the four kinds of precious substances and where the ground procures the **delightful sensation**[62] of **giving slightly** when trodden underfoot and **leaving an imprint** when one lifts one's foot, because of one's deeds **one is again stricken by the terrible suffering of wandering** in agony in hell, knee deep in **burning embers**, and through swamps of **rotting corpses** and excrement. **I beg you to** bear this in mind and **think**, "I will have to experience that."

(iv) How there is no essence to happy activities

Those who in the Joyous Garden played,
And in Beauty's Grove were served by heaven's maids,
Will come to woods of trees with swordlike leaves
And cut their hands and feet, their ears and nose. (72)

Among the golden lotuses and lovely maids
They bathed in heaven's Gently Flowing Pool,
But into hell's own waters will they plunge,
The scalding, caustic River None Can Ford. (73)

Having **delighted** at length in the pleasures of the desire realm, **arriving in the Garden of Joy and the Grove of Utter Beauty** surrounded by many **attentive daughters** of the gods **in the higher realms, again**, in hell, one will arrive **in the forest of swordlike leaves**, with pointed stakes and a variety of sharp weapons for leaves, stirred by the wind. As, driven by karma, one climbs up and falls down, **one will cut one's hands and feet, ears and nose**, and undergo all sorts of sufferings having one's whole body and limbs slashed and pierced.

One might have spent a long time experiencing the pleasures of **entering** the celestial pool, the **Gently Flowing**, surrounded by **the beautiful faces of the daughters of the gods**, and bathing in its **golden lotus-filled** waters, which have the eight perfect qualities. **But know that afterwards** there is no doubt **one will again** have to **plunge into the intolerable, scalding hot alkaline waters of hell's unfordable river** of hot ashes, the Vaitarani.[63]

(v) How there is no essence to great wealth

> A Kamaloka god, one gains such bliss,
> As Brahma, bliss that's free from all desire;
> But know that after that comes constant pain:
> As firewood one feeds Avici's flames. (74)

One might have obtained the immense happiness of the world of desire, living in **the gods' realms** above the Heaven Free of Conflict—a sublime happiness much greater than that in the gods' realms below; **or** obtained **the bliss free from** the **attachment** of the world of desire in **Brahma**'s world, the world of form. But **know that afterwards**, because of one's "negative deeds due to be experienced in other lives,"[64] **one will** have to **endure the ceaseless suffering of being** horribly burnt as if one were **fuel for the fires of the Hell of Torment Unsurpassed**.

(vi) How great splendor cannot be relied on

> One who was reborn as sun or moon,
> Whose body's light lit whole worlds far below,
> Will then arrive in states of darkest gloom,
> His outstretched hands will be invisible. (75)

One might have obtained rebirth as a child of the gods, as **the sun or the moon itself**, which the Tirthikas believe to be gods; **with the light of one's own body** (or, as commonly recounted **on earth,** with the celestial measureless palace)[65] one **illuminated the whole** world below. But even having been so bright and luminous, **again one will reach,** or take birth in, the **pitch darkness** between worlds, where there is no light from the sun or moon, **and** one will experience the misery of being in a place where one **cannot even see one's own hands stretched out** in front.

(2) Advice on recognizing all this and practicing virtue

So thus it is you'll ail, and knowing this
Please seize the lamp of merit's triple form,
For otherwise you'll plunge and go alone
In deepest dark unlit by sun or moon. (76)

Knowing that you will ail thus (meaning "die"), experiencing in a variety of ways such things as the impermanence of life and falling into lower states after staying in the higher realms, **firmly seize the light of the lamp** that dispels the darkness of the lower realms, **the three kinds of merit**—those that come from generosity, discipline, and meditation or those related to the body, speech, and mind. **Know that** without merit to light the way, **you will plunge alone**, with no one to accompany you, **into the darkness** of the three lower realms **on which** the light of **the sun and moon makes no impression**—they are powerless to overcome it. As it is said in the *Lalitavistara Sutra*:

Excepting all our virtuous deeds,
Which will follow and accompany us,
In compounded existences there's no companion,
No other refuge, friend, or retinue.

ii. Showing the huge extent of suffering

(1) Recognizing that samsara is by nature suffering

(a) The sufferings in the hells

(i) Brief introduction

For beings who indulge in evil deeds
There's constant pain in these and other hells:
Reviving Hell, Black Line, and Intense Heat,
And Crushing, Screaming, Torment Unsurpassed. (77)

Sentient beings who perform negative actions with their body, speech, and mind **will experience** the sufferings of the hells. What are these sufferings? They are the **constant torments** that will be experienced **in the Reviving Hell, Black Line Hell,** Hell of Heat, **Hell of Intense Heat, Crush-**

ing Hell, Screaming Hell, Great Screaming Hell, and the **Hell of Torment Unsurpassed,**[66] **and others**, that is, the neighboring hells, the ephemeral hells, and the eight cold **hells**.

(ii) Detailed explanation

[1] The sufferings one needs to know

[a] The actual sufferings

> Some are squeezed and pressed like sesame,
> Others likewise ground like finest flour,
> Some are cut and carved as if with saws,
> Others hacked with axes, razor-honed. (78)
>
> Others still are forced to swallow draughts
> Of burning molten bronze that flares and sparks,
> Some impaled and threaded onto skewers—
> Barbed and fiercely blazing stakes of steel. (79)
>
> Some, whom savage dogs with iron fangs
> Will rip to shreds, in dread throw up their hands,
> And others, powerless, are pecked by crows
> With sharpened beaks of steel and razor claws. (80)
>
> Some there are who roll about and wail,
> Devoured by worms and multicolored grubs,
> Ten thousand buzzing flies and bees that leave
> Great stings and bites unbearable to touch. (81)
>
> Some, in heaps of blazing red hot coals,
> Are burned without a break, their mouths agape.
> And some are boiled in cauldrons made of iron,
> Cooked like dumplings, heads turned upside down. (82)

First, the Crushing Hell, a hot hell. **Some** beings are **squeezed as if** in an iron press used for extracting **sesame** oil, causing putrid blood to flow out. **Similarly, other** beings in this hell are **ground** by blazing iron mills and mortars and reduced to **fine flour, like** that of rice or other grains. **Some** beings, in the Black Line Hell, are **carved up as if by** blazing **saws, others,**

likewise, chopped up with fiery **axes with excruciatingly sharp blades. Similarly, others** in the Hell of Heat or on the banks of the Unfordable River, their mouths forced open with iron tongs, **are given liquid of burning molten bronze wreathed with fiery** sparks **to drink**. In the Hell of Heat, **some are skewered on barbed, fiercely blazing stakes of steel.**

In the Forest of Swordlike Leaves, **some** have their bodies **torn to pieces** and devoured **by fierce steel-fanged hounds** barking loudly, **and throw their hands up in the air**, crying out for help. **Other helpless** beings at the top of the hill of shalmali trees have their eyes pecked out and flesh **torn away by** flocks of **crows** and other birds **with sharp steel beaks** and **mercilessly** sharp iron **claws**.

Some are eaten by the **worms** in their own bodies, by **insects of various** species, colors and shapes, **and by** many **tens of thousands of bluebottles and black bees inflicting great bites, which are exquisitely painful to touch.** Because of this, **they roll** their bodies on the ground, their voices **wailing in distress**. This is a suffering in the neighboring hells.

Some beings in the Hell of Heat are **burned uninterruptedly in piles of glowing** iron **embers** by the guardians of hell and have no strength but to lie with their **mouths stretched open**. And **some** in that hell are cooked **upside down in huge cauldrons made of iron**, filled with brine and blazing with fire—**cooked like rice dumplings**, which, when thrown into a pot of boiling water, are alternately sucked down and thrown up to the surface again.

[b] How and to whom these sufferings happen

[i] Reflecting on when these sufferings befall one

> The very instant that they cease to breathe
> The wicked taste the boundless pains of hell.
> And he who hearing this is not afraid
> A thousandfold is truly diamond hard. (83)

Evil beings who have committed acts whose result will definitely be experienced as the suffering of the hells go to hell **in just** the time it takes to **breathe in and out**, because there is only the merest **interval** in which they proceed to hell: they are reborn there the moment breathing stops. **Anyone** whose mind **is not terrified a thousand times over**, and whose body does not crack into a thousand pieces **on hearing of their immeasurable** or infinite **suffering in hell**, definitely has a body and mind **as hard as a diamond**, because otherwise he would be much more afraid.

[ii] Reflecting on how unbearable these sufferings are when they occur

– In general

> If simply seeing pictures of the hells
> And hearing, thinking, reading of them scares,
> Or making sculpted figures, need we say
> How hard to bear the ripened fruit will be? (84)

If even seeing drawings of the hells, or hearing about them from others **and** in that way **thinking about them**, **or reading** books containing passages from the sutras and so on, **or representing them** with materials such as clay **will make one afraid, one need hardly mention** the actual **experience, the** utterly **terrible fully ripened effect.**

– Showing in particular how the suffering in the Hell of Torment Unsurpassed is greater than all sufferings

> Of all the forms of happiness there are,
> The lord is bliss where craving's fully spent.
> So too, of all the misery there is,
> The pain in Torment Unsurpassed is worst. (85)

Just as of all kinds of happiness it is complete liberation, or **the lord of bliss, the** complete **exhaustion of the craving** of the three worlds, that **is considered** supreme, **of all sufferings the suffering in the Hell of Torment Unsurpassed is by far the** greatest and the **most terrible.**

– An example showing how the torment of hell is much greater even than the especially great pain of being struck by common weapons

For one whole day on earth three hundred darts
Might strike you hard and cause you grievous pain,
But that could never illustrate or match
A fraction of the smallest pain in hell. (86)

The pain for a whole day, here among humans, **of being struck with very great force by three hundred short spears** at once **does not even** begin to **hint** at the sufferings of just the ephemeral hells, **the smallest of hell's sufferings**: an example such as this **does not compare with so much as a fraction**, a hundred-thousandth of those torments.

[iii] Reflecting on how long one experiences them

The frightful pains and torments just described
Are lived and felt throughout a billion years.
Until those evil deeds are fully spent
One will not die and shed this life in hell. (87)

The utterly terrible sufferings just described are experienced for billions of years, and as long as those negative actions have not been exhausted one will not die. The extent of each of these is described in the *Treasury of the Abhidharma*:

In the six hells, Reviving and the others, respectively,
One day equals a lifetime as a Kamaloka god.
Their respective life spans resemble
Those in the Kamaloka god realms.[67]

and

Intense Heat is half and Torment Unsurpassed a whole
Intermediate kalpa.

As long as one stays there one will experience hell, because the power of the action that becomes that experience has not been exhausted.

[2] Advice on avoiding the causes of these sufferings

The seeds of these the fruits of evil deeds
Are sinful acts of body, speech, and mind.
Work hard therefore and muster all your skill
To never stray a hair's breadth into sin. (88)

The seeds of these torments in hell, which are the **results of negative actions, are** the three kinds of **wrong conduct with the body** (taking life and so forth), the four with **speech** (telling lies and so on) **and** the three with the **mind** (covetousness and the others), on a large, medium, or small scale. O King, **you must, by all means, never do even an atom's worth of these** three kinds of negative action. **Endeavor in this very thing with all your** mental **skill.**

(b) The sufferings of the animals

(i) General sufferings

For animals there's multifold distress—
They're slaughtered, tied up, beaten, and the rest.
For those denied the virtue that brings peace
There's agony as one devours another. (89)

Throughout the animal realm too there is an infinite **variety of suffering.** Animals are **killed** by other beings, human and otherwise, **trussed up** with lassos and the like, **beaten** and whipped, and they suffer all sorts of other injury from humans and nonhumans. Being reborn as unsuitable vessels, animals **are unable to practice**[68] **the** sublime **virtue**[69] and so on **by which one will** obtain the **peace** of nirvana, and they are certain to **have the truly horrendous** ripened effect of **being eaten by one another**.

(ii) The specific sufferings of animals that live scattered in different places

Some of them are killed just for their pearls,
Their wool, or bones, their meat or skins and fur,
And other helpless beasts are forced to work,
They're kicked or struck with hands, with whips and goads. (90)

Some animals living in the sea **are killed** for **pearls**, some, such as sheep, for **wool;** elephants and so forth for their **bones**; deer and other wild ungulates for their **meat**; **and** some, such as tigers and leopards, **on account of their skins**. **Other** animals—horses, buffaloes, donkeys, oxen, elephants, and the like—owned by gods and men **have no freedom of their own** and suffer from being **forced into service and struck** with weapons, being respectively **kicked, hit, whipped, and goaded**.

(c) The sufferings of the pretas

(i) Brief introduction

> For pretas too there's not the slightest break
> In suffering from their unfulfilled desires.
> What dire misery they must endure
> From hunger, thirst, cold, heat, fatigue, and fear. (91)

For beings born as **pretas there are the sufferings produced by frustrated desires**. And because these are **constant** and **unchanging**, and there is no way to stop them, **you should know** that the pretas will undoubtedly have to **endure the most terrible** misery **arising from hunger and thirst, from cold** in winter **and heat** in summer, **exhaustion** from searching for food and drink, **and terror** when they see people brandishing sharp weapons and so forth. The point here is that you have to be diligent now in practicing positive actions assiduously.

(ii) Detailed explanation

[1] The suffering

[a] The actual suffering

> Some, their mouths like needles' eyes, their bellies
> Huge as mountains, ache from want of food.
> They do not even have the strength to eat
> Discarded scraps, the smallest bits of filth. (92)

Some, their naked bodies skin and bone,
Are like the dried-out tops of tala trees.
And some have mouths that belch forth fire by night:
Into their burning mouths sand falls as food. (93)

A few unlucky ones don't even find
Some dirt to eat—pus, excrement, or blood.
They hit each other in the face and eat
The pus that festers from their swollen necks. (94)

For hungry ghosts the summer moon's too hot,
In wintertime the sun is far too cold,
Fine trees in orchards wilt and lose their fruit,
And simply from their gaze great streams run dry. (95)

Some pretas **have mouths as small as the eye of a needle, while their stomachs are** as big as **a mountain in size** and difficult to fill so that **they are tormented by hunger. Even** if they find **a little bit of discarded filth**—excrement, urine, and the like—their mouths are so small **they do not have the strength to eat** it.

Some have **bodies** that are simply **skin and bone**, without any flesh, and are **naked** because they have no clothes. They are **like the dried top of a palmyra tree**, without any bark.[70] **Some blaze** fire **from their mouths** every **night**—though not during the day—**and eat** hot **sand as food that falls into their burning mouths.**

Some of the most wretched kinds of pretas, with extremely little merit, suffer when they **fail to find even filth such as pus, excrement, or blood,** so one need hardly mention what it is like for them not finding anything good to eat. And yet, when they see each other **they** become enraged, **hit each other on the face** and throw clubs, bruising their **necks** and causing **carbuncles to appear. The ripened pus** dripping from these is what they have to endure as food.

These inferior classes of **pretas** suffer greatly from heat and cold: **in summertime even the moon is too hot for them, while in winter they are cold even in the sun. Orchard trees,** merely on being looked at by these pretas, appear to **lose their** ripe, abundant **fruit** and wither. And on account of their actions, **their mere gaze makes rivers** endowed with the eight perfect qualities seem to **dry up** and become filled with burning embers and quantities of excrement crawling with worms, "because," as we read in the sutras, "there is one reality but a variety of minds." *Introduction to the Middle Way* has this to say:

> *A preta will perceive a river as a stream of pus.*
> *Briefly, just as knowledge objects, so the mind—*
> *It should be understood that both are inexistent.*[71]

And in *The Way of the Bodhisattva* we read:

> *Who has forged this burning iron ground?*
> *Whence have all these demon women sprung?*
> *All are but the offspring of the sinful mind,*
> *Thus the Mighty One has said.*[72]

[b] The length of time their suffering is experienced

> And some have bodies bound by that tight noose,
> Their karmic store of previous evil deeds,
> Now borne as constant misery and pain;
> For five, ten thousand years they will not die. (96)

Some beings bound by the tight karmic noose of negative actions, which are endured in subsequent lives **as** continuous **suffering without** the slightest **break** or opportunity for happiness, **will not die for five thousand or even ten thousand years**, even though they have no food or drink in all that time. Thus will they suffer on account of their actions.

[2] The cause for experiencing these sufferings

> The cause of these the pretas' varied woes
> And all such kindred torments one might get
> Is being greedy, this the Buddha said:
> Stinginess is not for the sublime. (97)

The cause of anything one obtains that is similar to the misery that the pretas experience **in this way**—the **various** sufferings of hunger and thirst—**is someone who indulges in avarice** and is habitually stingy. **The Buddha said that** to be **miserly is not** the way of the **sublime** beings, as we read in the *Condensed Prajñaparamita Sutra*:

The miserly will be born among the pretas,
And even if born as humans, they will lead a life of poverty.

(d) The sufferings of the gods

(i) Brief introduction

Even in the higher realms the pains of death
Are more intense than is their greatest bliss.
And so good people who reflect on this
Don't crave the higher realms, which soon must end. (98)

One might obtain rebirth **in the higher realms** as a god in the world of desire. **But** though the gods are indeed **very happy** and enjoy abundance and perfection in a desirable place, **their anguish** when they go through the experience of **death and transmigration is much greater** even than the happiness they had before. As it is said:

"Alas, the Grove of Many-Colored Chariots,
Alas, the Gently Flowing Pool,
Alas, the gods we hold so dear!"
Thus they wail and fall to the ground.

Having reflected on this, good people who have knowledge, realization, and wisdom do not crave happiness, for even happiness **will be exhausted**: it has no true essence, and for this reason they **do not crave the** happiness of the **higher realms**.

(ii) Detailed explanation

Their bodies' colors cease to charm and please,
Their seats grow hard, their flowered wreaths do wilt,
Their clothes are stained, and on their bodies now appear
Rank drops of sweat they never had before. (99)

These five are signs that herald death in heaven,
Appearing to the gods in their abodes.
They're not unlike the signs of death that warn
Of coming death in humans on the earth. (100)

Those gods who transmigrate from heavenly worlds
And do not have some little virtue left
Will tumble, helpless, to their just abodes
As beasts or hungry spirits or in hell. (101)

If the gods, being miraculously born, do not suffer from dying, how then do they suffer? Their anguish is mental: when the time comes for gods to die, (1) **their** beautiful **complexions** fade and they **grow ugly**; (2) their **seats** become **uncomfortable** to sit on; (3) the **garlands of flowers** with which they are adorned **grow old**; (4) **stains appear on their garments**; and (5) **sweat, hitherto absent, now breaks out on their bodies** and they smell foul. These **five signs of death that herald death and transmigration in the higher realms** (meaning the god realms) **occur for the gods living in the god realms** of the world of desire, and **are similar to the signs of death**—the stench of death and so on—**that announce approaching death in humans on earth.**

For those who have died and **transmigrated from the worlds of the gods, if they have no remaining positive actions** that will lead to their taking birth in the higher realms, **then, powerless, they will** experience the sufferings, **whichever they may be, of the animal, preta, or hell realms.**

(e) The sufferings of the asuras

The asuras begrudge the gods their splendor,
Their inbred loathing thus torments their minds.
Though clever, they're obscured as all their kind,
And so it is they cannot see the truth. (102)

Even in the abodes of **the asuras, on account of** their extreme pride and their **natural hatred for the gods** and their **splendor**, they **suffer greatly mentally**, for their jealousy makes them unhappy. Moreover, when they engage in battle with the gods they suffer further from their physical injuries. **Although they have** the **intelligence** to distinguish positive and negative actions, **they have the obscurations** (the fully ripened effect of past actions) **of beings** who have not seen the truth. **For this reason, they are unable to see the truth** in their current body,[73] because this kind of support is incompatible with seeing the truth. In the commentaries it is explained that rebirth as an asura is propelled by a negative action and completed by a positive action, but Arya Asanga says that because asuras are celestial beings they are propelled by a positive propelling action.[74]

(2) The need, once one recognizes that samsara is suffering, for effort in order to stop rebirth

(a) The reason one has to stop rebirth

> Samsara is like this, and thus we are reborn
> As gods, as humans, denizens in hell,
> As ghosts or animals; but you should know
> That birth's not good, a pot of many ills. (103)

Because samsara has defects **like these**, as has been explained, **one takes birth**, as a result of actions and afflictive emotions, in the bodies of **gods, humans, hell beings, pretas, and animals. Know**, says Nagarjuna, **that rebirth** in those states **is not good: they are vessels for much harm.**

(b) Advice on making every effort to stop birth for this very reason

> Give up your efforts trying to stop all this
> As if your hair or clothes had just caught fire;
> Just do your best to not be born again:
> No greater goal or need is there than this. (104)

Unlike **someone whose hair or clothes have suddenly caught fire** desperately trying to put out the flames quickly, be wise: in recognizing the defects of samsara, **give up making** any effort **to put an end to the latter and rather**, without regard for life or limb, diligently **put your efforts** into **not being reborn again**, because **there is no greater purpose** for a person **than** to put an end to rebirth.[75]

B. How to truly set out towards perfect enlightenment[76]

1. Having confidence in liberation, the result

> With discipline and concentration, wisdom too,
> Attain nirvana, peaceful, disciplined, immaculate,
> Unageing, deathless, inexhaustible, and quite distinct
> From earth and water, fire, wind, sun, and moon. (105)

By means of the three trainings explained earlier, namely the trainings in **discipline, concentration, and wisdom**, you should attain the **stainless** state unsullied by afflictive emotions—both the **nirvana** without residue that is **peaceful** because the tainted aggregates have been brought to cessation, and the nirvana with residue, in which the senses are **controlled**. Since its youthfulness does not change, **it is unageing**; since its life force does not alter, it is **deathless**; and since it never runs out, it is **inexhaustible**. Some non-Buddhists assert that liberation has material form:

> *Like snow, like conch, like incense smoke,*
> *Like curd or cows or pearls its hue,*
> *And like a white umbrella is its shape—*
> *Such is liberation, the Jaina has explained.*[77]

But Nagarjuna shows that liberation is not as they claim. In order to refute liberation with a shape, and to help those who believe in **earth, water, fire, wind**, the sun, and moon as sources of refuge to give up such beliefs, he says, "**attain freedom from** the belief in **the sun and moon** as a refuge."

2. Practicing the truth of the path, the cause

a. The path of seeing

i. The essence of the path, seven elements leading to enlightenment

> Mindfulness, discernment, diligence, a joyful mind,
> And flexibility, concentration, evenness—
> These seven limbs are elements that lead to Buddhahood,
> They gather virtue and attain the state beyond all pain. (106)

On the path of seeing there is (1) **mindfulness** whereby one does not forget the object, the truth; (2) the wisdom of **perfect discernment** with regard to the object; (3) **diligence**, delight in virtue, being assiduous in undertaking what is right and avoiding what is wrong in accordance with the path; (4) **joy** or mental happiness regarding the latter; (5) **flexibility**, in which mind and body function appropriately; (6) **concentration**; **and** (7) **evenness**, in which the mind enters the natural state, free from the conditions of lack of clarity and wildness. **These seven are elements of** the path of seeing, the essence of **enlightenment. They** will **make one accumulate** or accomplish **the positive actions that help one attain nirvana.**

ii. A specific explanation of the profound yoga of wisdom related to sustained calm

(1) Brief introduction

> Lacking wisdom, concentration fails,
> And without concentration, wisdom too.
> For someone who has both, samsara's sea
> Fills no more than the print left by a hoof. (107)

Without the **wisdom** that understands correctly the particular and general characteristics of phenomena **there is no** developing **concentration**, because it is necessary to concentrate in meditation on a subject that has been understood through wisdom.[78] **Again, without concentration there is not the wisdom** that knows the nature of things, because it has been said by the Buddha that it is from settling the mind in meditation that one has the perfect knowledge of things as they are. **Know that for a** yogi **who has both** one-pointed concentration and the wisdom that knows how things truly are, **the ocean of existence is like** the water in **a hoofprint,** and as easily crossed. By wisdom is meant the correct realization of the no-self of the individual and the no-self of phenomena, because nothing else can completely destroy existence. Thus without wisdom concentration will go astray, but without concentration there is no benefit from having wisdom alone. So by completing the path of sustained calm and profound insight combined, one attains nirvana. Of these, profound insight is more important than sustained calm, which is why it is said by those who praised the Buddha's teachings:

> *Because they do not follow your teaching,*
> *Ignorant, blind individuals,*
> *Even having reached the peak of existence,*
> *Suffer again and accomplish existence.*

and,

> *Those who follow your teaching,*
> *Though they might not attain the main concentration,*
> *Will put an end to existence*
> *Even under the demons' watchful eyes.*

(2) Detailed explanation

(a) What one has to abandon: views on which the Buddha did not give an opinion, and which are incorrect approaches to the way things are

> The Kinsman of the Sun did well pronounce
> With silence on the fourteen worldly points.
> On these you must not ponder or reflect,
> With them your mind will never be at peace. (108)

The Buddha Bhagavan, the **Friend of the Sun,**[79] in his teachings perfectly **pronounced on fourteen points about the world on which he did not give an opinion.**[80] **These** are as follows:

- Four that relate to parinirvana: that a Buddha, beyond death, exists; that he does not exist; that he both exists and does not exist; or that he neither exists nor does not exist.

- Four that relate to the past: that the self and the world are eternal, impermanent, both, or neither.
- Four that relate to the future: that the self and the world have an end, do not have an end, have both, or have neither.
- And two that relate to body and life: is a given body a life, or is the body different from the life?

There is no need to answer such questions because the subject,[81] permanence, does not exist, and therefore its properties[82] cannot exist either, so there is no point in answering.[83] Here "life" is a synonym of "self."

Why are these referred to as "points on which the Buddha did not give an opinion?" When certain non-Buddhists asked the Tathagata about these points, he, knowing that their question had as its premise a permanent self, did not pronounce on its being permanent, impermanent, or otherwise because he thought that it would be inappropriate to examine the properties of a nonexistent subject.[84] At the same time he thought it would not be helpful to refute the subject saying, "the basis of predication does not exist." So he said nothing. This is why we speak of "points on which the Buddha did not give an opinion."

There is another explanation, as follows. The self is the individual labelled in dependence on the aggregates. The world is the five causal aggregates. Because these arise interdependently they have no intrinsic nature, and for this reason they do not exist as permanent or impermanent or otherwise. As it is said:

> *Anything that arises interdependently*
> *Is devoid of any essential nature.*

Therefore they are not to be taught as being permanent, impermanent, or anything else. Since the Tathagata considered the questioners to be unsuitable vessels for the profound teachings he did not teach interdependence as being devoid of intrinsic nature either. So this is why these topics are referred to as "points on which the Buddha did not give an opinion." *The Jewel Garland* states:

> *If asked whether the world has an end,*
> *The Victorious One will remain silent.*
> *Why? Subjects as profound as that*
> *He does not teach to unsuitable vessels.*

This is because, the wise know well,
The All-Knowing One is omniscient.

Do not reflect on these views, believing that there is some truth in them, because if one is impregnated with the poison of wrong views, the poison of afflictive emotions will proliferate. **This** thinking about them **is not** the way to liberate **the mind in peace**: the intellect will become confused and the mind infertile.

(b) The antidote: the true mode of being that is interdependence

(i) Interdependence[85]

From ignorance comes action, and from that
Comes consciousness, thence name-and-form appears.
From that arise the six sense faculties,
Whence contact comes, thus did the Buddha teach. (109)

And then from contact feeling comes to be,
And based on feeling, craving will appear.
Again from craving grasping will be born,
And then becoming, and from this there's birth. (110)

Then once there's birth, comes misery untold,
And sickness, ageing, wants frustrated, death,
Decay, in short the whole great mass of pain.
If birth is stopped, all this will be no more. (111)

In the *Sutra of Interdependence* the Bhagavan states:

O Monks, if there is this, this will come about.
Because this has taken birth, this will be born.
Thus, because of the condition of ignorance, there are
conditioning factors ... (and so on),
Because of the condition of birth there is ageing-and-death,
And misery, lamenting, unhappiness, and conflict.
Thus there will arise this great mass that is only suffering.

and,

> *Likewise by stopping ignorance one stops conditioning factors,*
> *And so by stopping birth ageing-and-death, misery,*
> *Lamenting, unhappiness and conflict are all stopped.*
> *Thus this great mass of suffering will be stopped.*

What does this mean? **From ignorance**, the view that the aggregates are or belong to the self, what we call "action"—meritorious, nonmeritorious, and unwavering[86]—arises, and **from action** the **consciousness** that seizes a birth with habitual karmic tendencies is born. According to the *Verses on Interdependence*, the consciousness first enters the mother's womb. **From that** consciousness, the five aggregates of the embryo and other stages **are fully produced** as **name and form**, the latter being a combination of the elements and their compounds.[87] Then, as that "name-and-form" grows, **the six** inner **sense powers**, such as that of the eye, are produced; **and from these** six sense powers, **contact** (which is the coming together of object, organ, and consciousness) **occurs, as the Capable One has declared**.

From contact, a **feeling** of happiness or suffering **arises, and based on** that **feeling there comes craving**—accepting some things because one wants to be happy and rejecting others because one wants to avoid being unhappy. When **craving**, which initiates the acceptance of happiness and the rejection of suffering, increases greatly, **grasping is born. Then from that** grasping, the capacity of revived habitual karmic tendencies to take rebirth becomes very powerful and **becoming** will occur. **From becoming comes birth** in the next life.

Once there is birth, misery occurs, tormenting the body and mind; there is **illness** as changes in one's constitution occur; **ageing** as one's youthfulness alters; **frustrated desire** for things like food and clothes; **death** when one's life force changes; **and** physical **decay** beyond one's own control, and **other** difficulties **as a result** of which one laments vocally and feels unhappy mentally, and so forth. Thus there comes about **the whole enormous mass of suffering**. Now by putting an end to the root (i.e., ignorance), conditioning factors are stopped, and by halting them, consciousness and the others are halted; and **by halting birth, all this**—ageing and the rest—**will be brought to an end**.

How long does it take to complete a cycle of these twelve interdependent links? No more nor less than three lifetimes. Thus, ignorance, conditioning factors, and consciousness are completed in a previous life, because they are the propellers for taking birth. The links from name-and-form through to feeling are completed in the middle life, because they are by their nature the fully ripened effect. Craving, grasping, and becoming are also completed in the middle life, because they are fully ripened effects that arise from conditions. Birth and ageing-and-death are completed in the next life, because the last link in this life is becoming and birth is to be accomplished as a result of the latter. Further, as a result of birth, ageing-and-death occur.

In this scheme of things, the first two lives do not necessarily occur contiguously, because it is possible for one's present name-and-form to have been propelled by ignorance and so on dating from more than a hundred kalpas in the past. In the case of the fully ripened effect of an "action whose effect is definitely to be experienced in the next life,"[88] it is possible for the first two lives to occur one after the other without intervening lives. The last two lives are necessarily contiguous, because birth and ageing-and-death in the next life arise as a result of becoming in this life. For this reason, birth and ageing-and-death in this life do not belong to the same cycle of interdependent links as this life's name-and-form and so on, for they do not arise as a result of this life's craving and grasping. What, then, does happen? They belong to the same cycle as the previous life's name-and-form, because this life's birth and ageing-and-death arise as a result of the craving, grasping, and becoming in that previous life.

Thus childish beings have all twelve interdependent links even in this present life, but these are a combination of interdependent links belonging to three lives, past, middle, and future. In this case, ageing-and-death belongs to a previous cycle. Ignorance, conditioning factors, and consciousness are the interdependent links belonging to the next cycle, because they are the propellers for birth in a future life. Name-and-form through to becoming are the interdependent links of this life.

Thus the twelve links present in this life are also what dispel confusion concerning past and future lives. Name-and-form through to feeling are the propelled results of a previous life; birth and ageing-and-death are the accomplished results: from these one can infer the existence of former lives. Ignorance, conditioning factors, and consciousness are the links that propel birth in a future life; craving, grasping, and becoming are the accomplishing causes: from these one can infer the existence of future lives. As one establishes how the twelve links present in this life are the original cause and end result of past and future lives, and one uses the same principles to work out the twelve interdependent links of past and future lives, one will fully appreciate how the twelve links of existence go round and round, with neither beginning nor end, like a whirling fire brand. As the Acharya[89] said:

> *From the three come two,*
> *From the two come seven, and the seven too*
> *Give rise to three; thus the wheel of existence*
> *Goes round and round, again and again.*

(ii) The importance of interdependence

> Within the treasury of Buddha's words
> There's none so precious, so profound as this.
> And those who see that things dependently arise
> Do see the Buddha, perfect knower of the truth. (112)

This principle of **dependent arising** that we have explained **is the most precious thing in the treasury of the Buddha's speech** because the essence of what all his teachings express can be condensed into adopting and avoiding, and dependent arising is what explains that. And it is on the basis of dependent arising that the Buddha taught the Middle Way, which is free from self and other, from both, and from eternalism and nihilism. It is **profound** and difficult for others to understand. **Those who correctly see this** dependent arising **see the Buddha, the sublime form of he who knows the true nature** of all things, for the Buddha is described in terms of the dharmakaya, which is no different from the natural state of interdependence. As it is said in the *Rice Seedling Sutra*:

> *They who know dependent arising know the Dharma,*
> *They who know the Dharma know the Tathagata.*

In other words, if one understands interdependence, one understands the Dharma of the Middle Way, which is free from eternalism and nihilism, and by putting that into practice one will attain Buddhahood.

b. The path of meditation

i. The essence of the path, the eightfold noble path

> Perfect view and livelihood, with effort,
> Mindfulness and concentration, perfect speech,
> And conduct, perfect thought—the path's eight limbs—
> To find true peace, please meditate on these. (113)

Right view, livelihood, effort, mindfulness, concentration, speech, conduct, and right thought are aspects **of**, and contributors to, **the** noble **path**.

- The noble path of right view is what was realized on the path of seeing, the wisdom that results from thorough, intelligent investigation.
- The noble path of right thought is the motivation to use one's speech to teach others according to one's own realization.
- The noble path of right speech is the verbal expression that issues from that realization in revealing the true nature of how things are.
- The noble path of right conduct is the physical and verbal expression related to avoiding anything that contravenes discipline, avoiding actions that do not respect the five basic vows.[90]
- The noble path of right livelihood is to clothe and feed oneself in accord with the Dharma.
- The noble path of right effort is to be diligent in meditation as the path.
- The noble path of right mindfulness is not to forget the object of meditation as the path.
- Right concentration is to remain one-pointed on that object of meditation.

At the stage of the path of meditation, **these eight elements** are parts of the noble path and contributors to it, and for this reason we speak of the eightfold noble path. So **in order to** attain **peace** (i.e., nirvana), **you must meditate** on them.

ii. How that constitutes the path

> To take birth is to suffer, and to crave
> Is its immense and universal source.
> Make craving cease and freedom will be yours,
> To achieve that take the Eightfold Noble Path. (114)

This birth, which is by nature the five causal aggregates, is **suffering**, as we find in the sutras:

> *In short, the five causal aggregates are suffering.*

What we call craving, which is attachment to the five tainted aggregates, **is the origin of that** suffering. As the Buddha said in a sutra:

> *What is the noble truth of the origin of suffering? Craving is the origin of suffering, together with attachment to delight, which seems to make one happy.*

This is the principal cause of birth in existence, and it is therefore **immense. Cessation**, whereby all these sufferings are brought to a halt, **is liberation, and** the path **for attaining that is this eightfold noble path** that has just been described.

iii. The most important thing on the path, the wisdom that sees the four truths

> For you to see these same Four Noble Truths
> You must strive hard to practice constantly. (115ab)

In order to see the ultimate nature of **these Four Noble Truths that have just been described, be diligent** in **constantly** practicing the path.

3. Encouragement for putting the above points into practice

a. Encouragement in terms of someone of modest potential accomplishing the practice

> Even worldly men with fortune in their laps,
> Through knowledge, crossed that river, troubled states;
> And even those who realized the truth
> Did not fall from the heavens, nor emerge
> Like crops of corn from earth's dark depths, but once
> Were ruled by kleshas and were ordinary men. (115cd, 116)

Even laymen such as King Bimbisara,[91] **in whose laps the splendor**—the wealth and fortune—of a kingdom reside, **have** seen the truth **through** perfect **knowledge** and **crossed the river of afflictive emotions.** So you too, O King, must do likewise, says Nagarjuna.

Not one of all the sublime beings who have appeared—**individuals who had** direct **realization of the Dharma** of the four truths—was already a sublime being right from the beginning: **they did not fall from the sky, nor did they emerge from the darkness of the earth like a crop. In the past they were subject to afflictive emotions**—they were **ordinary people** dominated by the afflictive emotions. They are therefore worth following as an example for accomplishing the path.

b. Encouragement in terms of essentializing the training

> O Fearless One, what need to tell you more?
> For here's the counsel that will truly help:
> The vital point is tame your mind, for mind's
> The root of Dharma, so the Buddha said. (117)

Intrepid One, says Nagarjuna addressing the king, for he has no fear of opponents, **why tell you too much?** There is no need. **The most essential**—the principal or most important—**instruction that benefits** both temporarily and ultimately **is this: tame your mind** by stopping negative actions and undertaking virtue. If you were to ask why, **the Bhagavan has declared the mind to be the root of the Dharma**. As it is said:

Mind it is that influences the world,
The mind that leads and guides it.
Because of this sole phenomenon—mind—
Come, following, all phenomena.[92]

and,

To tame the mind is excellent,
By taming mind one is led to peace.

c. Encouragement in terms of its being acceptable to practice according to one's ability

It's hard enough for monks to follow perfectly
All these instructions that I've given you.
Yet practice excellence, the very pith
Of one of these, and give your life its sense. (118)

O King, **it is difficult enough for fully ordained monks**, who apply themselves exclusively to positive actions, **to perfectly and completely carry out all the instructions that I have given you** above, so how could one expect laymen distracted by numerous activities to do so? Nevertheless, **the essence**, as it were, **of practicing** or accomplishing whatever you can of the main points **of these instructions is to rely on** and familiarize yourself with **good qualities, so by doing this make your life meaningful**. That way you will be following the Buddha's teaching and also gradually obtain other good qualities.

III. Epilogue

A. How to rejoice and dedicate

1. Dedication

> Rejoicing in the virtuous deeds of all,
> Now dedicate your three good kinds of acts
> To all that they may come to Buddhahood. (119abc)

Rejoicing in all the positive actions, tainted and untainted, **of all** beings, whether ordinary or sublime, may you **entirely dedicate the three kinds of positive deeds**—those performed with the body, speech, and mind—utterly purified of the three concepts[93] **in order that you may attain** perfect, infinite **Buddhahood** for the sake of others, so that through this mass of virtue, as long as the world lasts you will be its protector.

2. The result of that dedication

a. The temporary result

> Then by this mass of virtuous deeds may you,
> In boundless lives in worlds of gods and men,
> Be master of the yoga of all excellence,
> And like Sublime Chenrezig, may you work
> To guide the many feeble, stricken souls. (119d, 120)
>
> And thus may you take many rebirths and dispel all ills,
> Old age, desire, and hatred in a perfect Buddhafield. (121ab)

Subsequently, by this mass of virtue that has been dedicated, while you are practicing on the path, **in infinite lives**, being born **in the world of gods and men, may you master the yoga of all** the infinite qualities such as memory and concentration. **Then**, for the sake of others, **by acting** like **Arya Avalokiteshvara** and following his example in protecting destitute beings from all temporary and ultimate fears such as those of the eight and sixteen dangers—lions, elephants, and so forth, **may you guide** (by means of the Dharma) **many destitute beings stricken** by suffering, and complete the accumulations. And **having taken birth** again and again for the benefit of others until the end of existence, may you **dispel illness** and **ageing**

(which are included in the truth of suffering) and **attachment** and **aversion** (which are included in the origin of suffering), everything having been purified through your own sources of virtue into a **Buddhafield**.

b. The ultimate result: Buddhahood

> May you have infinite life, as a Protector of the World
> Like Buddha Amitabha, Sublime Lord of Boundless Light. (121cd)

Were one to ask whom one will be like, Nagarjuna anwers: **May you be the Protector of the** three **worlds, like the Buddha Amitabha,** remaining as long as samsara endures, **in infinite** realms, with infinite disciples, infinite **life span,** and so forth.

B. Summarizing everything as the result of the above path

> And springing from your wisdom, discipline, and bounty, may
> your fame
> And stainless virtues spread throughout the gods' realms,
> in the sky
> And on the earth, and may you firmly quell the carefree ways
> Of gods and men whose sole delight and joy is pretty girls. (122)
>
> And once you've reached the Mighty Buddha state, removing fear
> And birth and death for hosts of stricken and afflicted souls,
> Then let mere name be stilled, beyond the world, and reach
> The never-changing level, free from fear, that knows no wrong.
> (123)

Nagarjuna now sums up as follows. As a result of your **wisdom,** which is the realization of the natural state, your faultless **discipline** and **generosity**—from that perfect **source** may the **great fame** of your consummate splendor and the **immaculate** virtues of your body, speech, and mind (for they are devoid of negative action) **spread throughout the realms of the gods and in space and on the earth,** the human world. **Then** may you quell the **light-heartedness** and carefree ways **of men** living **on earth and** the six classes of **gods** of the world of desire **in the celestial realms,** who carelessly **indulge in pleasure** with **lovely young maidens;** may you establish them **firmly** on the path and lead them to nirvana, in which suffering has been **perfectly pacified.**

May you reach the state of the Mighty Buddha, one **who, for the host of sentient beings tormented by** suffering due to **afflictive emotions, removes fear** (due mainly to concrete views), **birth** (due principally to ignorance, actions, and craving) **and death** (when one's karma and life span run out and one is like a lost child abandoned by its parents). **Then** may you **pacify** all sufferings in the state **beyond the world,** which is the cessation of the five tainted aggregates and the unmistaken meaning of the true nature in which there has never been even the **mere name** of the relative. **Reach the level of fearlessness,** where all fear of existence has been eliminated, the state of **unchanging** youth, ever-untainted, the state **not subject to wrong** (i.e., death), for it is devoid of karmic obscurations, free of faults and unchanging, the state of the extraordinary and sublime nirvana.

Part Three

THE CONCLUSION

I. The author's name

> This completes the *Letter to a Friend* written by the Sublime Master Nagarjuna to a friend, King Surabhibhadra.

This **completes** the ***Letter to a Friend*** **by the** great **master** and protector of beings **Arya Nagarjuna**, one of the Six Ornaments who graced this world of Jambudvipa, who was resplendent with the major and minor marks of a Buddha and who spoke with the sixty branches of melodious speech. He **wrote** it to his **friend King Surabhibhadra**.

II. The translators' names

> It was translated, corrected, and authenticated by the learned Indian abbot Sarvajñanadeva and the great reviser and translator Venerable Paltsek.

The **learned Indian abbot Sarvajñanadeva** ("omniscient god") and the **great reviser and translator, the venerable** Kawa **Paltsek translated and corrected this and produced a definitive version**.

Letter to a Friend: Structural Outline

Part One INTRODUCTION
- I. The Title
  - A. Mentioning the Indian title
  - B. An explanation of the title in Tibetan
  - C. An explanation showing the correspondence between the two languages
  - D. A commentary on the meaning of the title
- II. The Translator's Homage

Part Two THE ACTUAL TEXT
- I. Prologue
  - A. Using the commitment to compose the text as an exhortation to listen **Verse 1**
  - B. A lesson in humility and why one should listen
    - 1. Humility with regard to the words **2**
    - 2. Humility with regard to the meaning **3**
- II. An explanation of the main text
  - A. An explanation of faith as a support on the path to the higher realms and lasting happiness
    - 1. Brief account of six things one should keep in mind, the Buddha and so forth, which are the basis of faith **4**
    - 2. Detailed explanation of the last three things to be kept in mind
      - a. Keeping celestial beings in mind **5**
      - b. Keeping bounteousness in mind **6**
      - c. Keeping discipline in mind **7**
  - B. An explanation of the essence of the path
    - 1. Brief introduction **8**

2. Detailed explanation: the six transcendent perfections
a. Generosity **9**
b. Discipline
i. Precepts that have to be kept **10, 11**
ii. Getting rid of incompatible traits **12**
iii. Exercising carefulness regarding what is compatible with discipline **13**
iv. An explanation, with examples, of the benefits of being careful **14**
c. Patience
i. An instruction on giving up anger (as a cause) **15**
ii. Giving up resentment (as a result) **16**
iii. In connection with this, a particular feature of the mind that is the basis for patience **17**
iv. Avoiding harsh words, the main condition that sparks off anger **18**
d. Diligence
i. The basis, what one should be diligent in **19**
ii. An instruction on diligence in matching intention and application **20**
e. Concentration
i. Preparation
(1) Avoiding distraction, which counters concentration
(a) Distraction by the object
(i) Controlling the senses by transforming one's inner thoughts
I. An instruction on guarding the senses from others' wives **21**
II. An instruction on guarding the senses from other desires **22**
III. The fault in not controlling the senses **23**
IV. In praise of those who are able to control their senses **24**
(ii) Getting rid of attachment by recognizing the characteristics of the object
I. Getting rid of attachment by fully recognizing that the chief source of desire in the world of desire is the female body **25**
II. Getting rid of attachment by understanding the way desire generally functions **26**
(b) Avoiding distraction by the eight ordinary concerns

(i) The antidote
I. The antidote itself **27**
II. The advantages of having the antidote and disadvantages of not having it **28**
(ii) An instruction on what to give up
I. The eight ordinary concerns that have to be given up **29**
II. Advice on giving up the negative actions that result from these
A. The advice itself **30**
B. Why it is necessary to avoid negative actions **31**
(c) Distraction by wealth
(i) A general explanation of the kinds of wealth to be adopted and abandoned **32**
(ii) Specific trivial pursuits to be given up **33**
(iii) The antidote to use for giving these up
I. The advantages of using the antidote **34**
II. The disadvantages of not having that antidote **35**
(d) Distraction by pleasurable indulgence
(i) Giving up attachment to one's spouse
I. Spouses to be avoided **36**
II. Those to be taken as a wife **37**
(ii) Giving up attachment to food **38**
(iii) Giving up attachment to sleep **39**
(2) Practicing the four boundless qualities as an aid to concentration **40**
ii. An instruction on the actual practice, meditating on the four concentrations **41**
iii. What is to be done in the postmeditation
(1) Positive and negative actions that have to be adopted or given up generally
(a) An explanation of the relative gravity of positive and negative actions **42**
(b) An instruction on cultivating powerful positive actions as antidotes to negative acts **43**
(2) How to avoid the things that hinder concentration in particular **44**

f. Wisdom

i. A brief account of the essence of the path with the five elements beginning with confidence

(1) Showing what one has to adopt: confidence and the other elements **45**

(2) What one has to abandon: how to get rid of arrogance by means of an antidote **46**

ii. Detailed explanation of wisdom: close mindfulness and the other elements

(1) Showing that wisdom is the root of all happiness in samsara and nirvana

(a) The right view of worldly people, which is the root of both higher rebirth and lasting happiness **47**

(b) The right supramundane view that leads to lasting happiness **48**

(2) The main explanation of the path endowed with such wisdom

(a) Specific explanations

(i) Ascertaining the no-self of the individual **49**

(ii) Investigating the aggregates that are the support of the self **50**

(b) The actual path

(i) An explanation of the three fetters, which are incompatible with the path **51**

(ii) An explanation of diligence, which is a favorable condition **52**

(iii) An explanation of the three trainings, the essence of the path

I. A general exposition of the three trainings **53**

II. A specific explanation of the training in wisdom

A. How to extract oneself from affliction

1. How to turn the mind away from the things of this life

a. Brief introduction **54**

b. Detailed explanation

i. Reflecting on the impermanence of life

(1) Meditating on impermanence by reflecting on the unpredictability of the time of death **55**

(2) Meditating on impermanence by reflecting on the inevitability of death **56**

(3) Meditating on impermanence by reflecting on other aspects **57**

(4) A concluding summary of the above **58**

ii. Reflecting on the difficulty of finding the freedoms and advantages

(1) How rare it is in general simply to be born as a human

(a) The rarity of a human birth **59**

(b) Showing how despicable it is to practice negative actions with such a body **60**

(2) Showing in particular the support endowed with the four wheels

(a) A general account of the four wheels as favorable conditions **61**

(b) A specific explanation of the spiritual friend **62**

(3) Reflecting on how to be free of the eight unfavorable conditions of lack of opportunity **63, 64**

2. *How to turn the mind away from the whole of samsara: reflecting on the defects of samsara*

a. Brief introduction **65**

b. Detailed explanation

i. How nothing can be relied on even if it looks like happiness

(1) How nothing can be relied on

(a) How, since one cannot be certain who is a friend and who an enemy, it is inappropriate to rely on anyone **66**

(b) How one can never be satisfied **67**

(c) How it is impossible to predict when it will all end **68**

(d) How one's position is uncertain and cannot be relied on

(i) How great dominion cannot be relied on **69**

(ii) How delightful company cannot be relied on **70**

(iii) How there is no essence to pleasant places **71**

(iv) How there is no essence to happy activities **72, 73**

(v) How there is no essence to great wealth **74**

(vi) How great splendor cannot be relied on **75**

(2) Advice on recognizing all this and practicing virtue **76**

ii. Showing the huge extent of suffering

(1) Recognizing that samsara is by nature suffering

(a) The sufferings in the hells

(i) Brief introduction **77**

(ii) Detailed explanation

- *[1] The sufferings one needs to know*
  - *[a] The actual sufferings* **78 - 82**
  - *[b] How and to whom these sufferings happen*
    - *[i] Reflecting on when these sufferings befall one* **83**
    - *[ii] Reflecting on how unbearable they are when they occur*
      - *In general* **84**
      - *Showing in particular how the suffering in the Hell of Torment Unsurpassed is greater than all sufferings* **85**
      - *An example showing how the torment of hell is much greater even than the especially great pain of being struck by common weapons* **86**
    - *[iii] Reflecting on how long one experiences them* **87**
- *[2] Advice on avoiding the causes of these sufferings* **88**

(b) The sufferings of the animals
- *(i) Showing their general sufferings* **89**
- *(ii) Reflecting on the specific sufferings of animals that live scattered in different places* **90**

(c) The sufferings of the pretas
- *(i) Brief introduction* **91**
- *(ii) Detailed explanation*
  - *[1] The suffering*
    - *[a] The actual suffering* **92 - 95**
    - *[b] The length of time their suffering is experienced* **96**
  - *[2] Showing the cause for experiencing these sufferings* **97**

(d) The sufferings of the gods
- *(i) Brief introduction* **98**
- *(ii) Detailed explanation* **99 - 101**

(e) The sufferings of the asuras **102**

(2) An instruction on the need, once one recognizes that samsara is suffering, for effort in order to stop rebirth
- *(a) The reason one has to stop rebirth* **103**

(b) Advice on making every effort to stop birth for this very reason **104**

B. Advice on how to truly set out towards perfect enlightenment

1. Having confidence in liberation, the result **105**

2. Practicing the truth of the path, the cause

a. An explanation of the path of seeing

i. An explanation of the essence of the path, seven elements leading to enlightenment **106**

ii. A specific explanation of the profound yoga of wisdom related to sustained calm

(1) Brief introduction **107**

(2) Detailed explanation

(a) An explanation of what one has to abandon: views on which the Buddha did not give an opinion, and which are incorrect approaches to the way things are **108**

(b) An explanation of the antidote: the true mode of being that is interdependence

(i) Interdependence **109 - 111**

(ii) Describing its importance **112**

b. An explanation of the path of meditation

i. The essence of the path, the eightfold noble path **113**

ii. An explanation of how that constitutes the path **114**

iii. An instruction on the most important thing on the path, the wisdom that sees the four truths **115ab**

3. Encouragement for putting the above points into practice

a. Encouragement in terms of someone of modest potential accomplishing the practice **115cd, 116**

b. Encouragement in terms of essentializing the training **117**

c. Encouragement in terms of its being acceptable to practice according to one's ability **118**

III. Epilogue
- A. An instruction on how to rejoice and dedicate
  - 1. Dedication **119abc**
  - 2. The result of that dedication
    - a. The temporary result **119d - 121ab**
    - b. The ultimate result: Buddhahood **121cd**
- B. An instruction summarizing everything as the result of the above path **122, 123**

Part Three THE CONCLUSION and completion of the text
- I. The author's name
- II. The translators' names

Notes

Note to the Translator's Introduction

1 Beings of modest capacity, who avoid negative actions and undertake positive actions in order to attain the higher realms; beings of middling capacity, who practice the path in order to attain liberation for themselves; and beings of greater capacity, who practice the path in order that they and all beings may attain perfect Buddhahood.

Note to the Root Text

1 As explained in the commentary, the fields are twofold and are therefore related to the fourth and fifth kind of deed.

Notes to the Commentary

1 Prakrit evolved from Sanskrit.

2 The words enclosed in parentheses here and in the following section are the only instances of additions made by the translator. As a rule, parentheses elsewhere in the translation have been used simply as punctuation devices and not to indicate an addition or comment by the translator.

3 According to some authorities, Nagarjuna also wrote the *Ratnavali* (*The Jewel Garland*) for him. Surabhibhadra is just one of several possible translations into Sanskrit of the king's name in Tibetan (*bde spyod bzang po*). See Translator's Introduction.

4 This paragraph specifies four general criteria characteristic of the translator's homage in such texts: by whom homage is paid, when, how, and why.

5 Skt. *arya giti.*

6 Tib. *gsung rab,* Skt. *pravacana,* the teachings of the Buddha.

7 "And so forth" refers in each case to the qualities of the Buddha, Dharma, and Sangha respectively as listed in the *Sutra Remembering the Three Jewels* (*Triratna-anusmrti-sutra, dkon mchog rjes dran*).

8 Tib. *bde 'gro*, i.e., as celestial beings or humans.

9 Lit. "in order to take their essence." There is a play on words here: "to take the essence of things that have no essence," in other words, to give meaning to things while bearing in mind that they are essentially void and meaningless.

10 These are the four "fields" (Tib. *zhing*): the field of good qualities, the field of suffering, the field of benefit, and the field of veneration (or offering).

11 "Pure conduct" (Tib. *tshang spyod*) is often used as a synonym for celibacy.

12 To make untrue claims that one has attained high realization or that one possesses supernatural powers is the most serious of lies and constitutes a root downfall of the pratimoksha vows.

13 In his commentary on Ngari Panchen's *Ascertaining the Three Vows* (*sdom gsum 'grel pa*), Dudjom Rinpoche points out that beings on the northern continent of Uttarakuru are not suitable supports for taking vows, unlike those on the other three continents of our world system (considered from the Buddhist cosmological point of view).

14 "Renewal and confession" (Tib. *gso sbyong*), also explained here as "nurturing and purifying," refers to the ritual of renewing one's vows and confessing downfalls. For laypeople observing this twenty-four-hour upavasa vow, the last two groups of three vows are considered together as a single vow, thus making eight vows in all.

15 I.e., the gods of the world of desire.

16 Angulimala (Tib. *sor phreng*) means "Finger Garland."

17 In *The Words of My Perfect Teacher* (p. 264) he is referred to as Shankara.

18 In this case, killing his mother, which is one of the five crimes with immediate retribution (see Glossary).

19 Lit. "like a ball of yarn," going down and bouncing straight up again like a ball of yarn used as a child's toy.

20 I.e., as a cause of patience.

21 I.e., the consequence of others' anger.

22 "Temporary" result as opposed to the ultimate result mentioned in the previous verse.

23 Shantideva, *The Way of the Bodhisattva*, translated by the Padmakara Translation Group (Boston: Shambhala, 1997), VI, 5 (end) and 6 (beginning).

24 Avoiding or giving up negative actions and adopting or undertaking positive actions.

25 For example, by recording it in notes, etc.

26 See the commentary on verse 21 above.

27 Tib. *snying po med pa;* i.e., there is nothing about the skin that could really be a cause for attachment, since like anything else that is subjected to proper analysis and broken down into its constituent elements, it is empty by nature.

28 *The Way of the Bodhisattva,* VIII, 65.

29 *The Way of the Bodhisattva,* VII, 9-10.

30 Vivid faith, eager or yearning faith, and confident faith. See *The Words of My Perfect Teacher,* pp. 171-172; *Treasury of Precious Qualities,* p. 124.

31 In the commentary these seven have been annotated with numbers to indicate the order in which they are more usually known: (1) faith, (2) discipline, (3) generosity, (4) learning, (5) a sense of shame, (6) a sense of decency, and (7) wisdom.

32 Tib. *'byor pa'i dgos pa ni chog shes pa yin pa'i phyir,* lit. "the reason one acquires things is to be content." If one is content with what one has, one will no longer feel any need to acquire more.

33 For them, the aggregates, which ordinary beings associate with the individual self, are simply phenomena like any other.

34 The realms of the first concentration in the world of form; see chart on pp. 184-185.

35 Tib. *bsam gtan,* Skt. *samadhi.* In this section Kangyur Rinpoche speaks of the "antidote branch" (Tib. *gnyen po'i yan lag*), which is one of the three branches of the four concentrations, each concentration being described here in terms of antidote, benefit, and condition, this last being in each case "concentration" in the sense of a mind focused one-pointedly (Tib. *sems rtse gcig pa*). The different aspects of the four samadhis described here are also dealt with in *Treasury of Precious Qualities,* pp. 240-241.

36 "Concentration" in this case translates the Tibetan term *ting nge 'dzin.*

37 "Pure" (Tib. *tshangs*) in this context can equally be translated by the Sanskrit *brahma.*

38 The four samadhis, the eight perfect freedoms, and other factors that lead to enlightenment. See *Treasury of Precious Qualities,* Appendix 9, pp. 341 et seq.

39 These are "elements" from among the thirty-seven elements of enlightenment, in this case the elements associated with the path of joining.

40 The sublime path comprises the path of seeing and the path of meditation. The supreme mundane level, as the final stage on the path of joining, is the point at which a Bodhisattva attains the path of seeing.

41 See chart on pp. 182-183 for a schematic presentation of the path of joining, of which this verse is an overview. The order in which the four stages of warmth, peak, acceptance, and supreme mundane level, and the two groups of five elements associated with them, are dealt with is not the usual one. Further clarification can be found in *Treasury of Precious Qualities*, pp. 302-303.

42 I.e., the thirty-seven elements leading to enlightenment (see chart on pp. 182-183). The four close mindfulnesses (related to the lesser path of accumulation) are referred to specifically in verse 54, while verse 48 describes the four aspects of the meditation associated with these. The elements of the path of joining were mentioned in verse 45, and those related to the path of seeing and the path of meditation will be described in verses 106 and 113 respectively. See also Appendix 6 in *Treasury of Precious Qualities*.

43 The three kinds of wisdom that come from listening, reflecting, and meditating.

44 The three types of suffering: the suffering of change, suffering upon suffering, and the all-pervading suffering of everything composite. See *The Words of My Perfect Teacher*, pp. 78-79 and *Treasury of Precious Qualities*, pp. 78-79.

45 In other words, the same statement made for each of the five aggregates (see Glossary, "Five aggregates").

46 I.e., the belief in a self.

47 Chandrakirti, *Introduction to the Middle Way*, translated by the Padmakara Translation Group (Boston: Shambhala, 2002), VI, 127. Kangyur Rinpoche has interpreted the last two lines of this verse somewhat differently from Mipham Rinpoche (in his commentary on the *Madhyamakavatara*). These lines have therefore been modified accordingly.

48 Tib. *dbang phyug*, the creator of the universe according to some ancient Indian philosophical systems.

49 The above is a highly condensed summary of Mahayana Buddhist arguments against the philosophical tenets of the principal non-Buddhist schools in ancient India. These arguments are developed in numerous Madhyamika texts. See, for example, Khenchen Kunzang Pelden and Minyak Kunzang Pelden,

Wisdom: Two Buddhist Commentaries, translated by the Padmakara Translation Group (St. Léon-sur-Vézère: Editions Padmakara), 1993, 1999.

50 Tib. *kun sbyor*. Jigme Khyentse Rinpoche explains these as afflictive emotions that make one "stick." *The Great Tibetan-Chinese Dictionary* (*bod rgya tshig mdzod chen mo*) describes them as being afflictive emotions because they "join or link one to suffering."

51 Tib. *bsam gtan bzhi'i ting nge 'dzin*.

52 Tib. *spong ba bdun*, the avoidance of the three negative actions of the body (killing, stealing, and sexual misconduct) and four negative actions of speech (lying, sowing discord, harsh speech, and worthless chatter).

53 Tib. *lhag pa'i sems*, lit. "superior mind" or "superior thoughts," defined as "superior to non-Buddhist concentration."

54 Tib. *kun nas nyon mongs phyogs*, refers to the first two truths, suffering and the cause of suffering.

55 This refers to the four close mindfulnesses, the first of the thirty-seven elements leading to enlightenment: mindfulness of the body, of feelings, of consciousness, and of mental objects.

56 A detailed account of the four great wheels is given in Chapter 5 of *Treasury of Precious Qualities*.

57 Khenpo Pema Sherab explains that "superior" (Tib. *lhag*) means here that the lama should have more knowledge than the disciple.

58 The results of the trainings in discipline, concentration, and wisdom are that one becomes respectively disciplined (Tib. *dul*), peaceful (Tib. *zhi ba*), and perfectly peaceful (Tib. *nye bar zhi ba*).

59 Central land, a place where one has access to the Buddha's teachings.

60 The four human rebirths with no opportunity to practice the Dharma are rebirth with wrong views, where there is no Buddha, as a barbarian, and dumb (mentally and physically).

61 The gods in the formless realm exist in a state of mental blankness, so although they are classed as sentient beings, they do not actually have the perception of being such.

62 Lit. the "bearable" pleasure (Tib. *bde ba bzod du rung ba*), in contrast with the "unbearable" (Tib. *mi bzad*) suffering in the last line of this verse.

63 Tib. *chu bo rab med pa*, the Unfordable River, Skt. *Vaitarani*.

64 I.e., the third category of actions classified according to whether their result is (1) experienced in the same life as that in which they are committed, (2) in the life immediately following it, or (3) in other subsequent lives. The second case refers to the five crimes with immediate retribution that result in rebirth in the Hell of Torment Unsurpassed as soon as one dies (see the story of Udayana on p. 91), but in the third case, as referred to in this verse, one has first reaped the fruit of some immensely powerful positive deed that has taken chronological precedence in its effect over that of a negative deed meriting rebirth in the Hell of Torment Unsurpassed.

65 According to Indian mythology the sun and moon are celestial beings whose bodies shine with light, but it was popularly held that the light that shines on the earth is the light from the base of the celestial palaces in which the sun and moon dwell.

66 Nagarjuna lists these hells in a different order than the usual one. Kangyur Rinpoche has therefore written numbers against their names in the text to correspond with their usual order: Reviving, Black Line, Crushing, Screaming, Great Screaming, Heat, Intense Heat, and Torment Unsurpassed.

67 This verse serves as a basis for calculating the life span in each of the first six hot hells, where one day in each hell is equal to a lifetime in the corresponding god realm in the world of desire (the Kamaloka), and the life span in each hell is equal in hell years to the number of god years of a god's lifetime in the corresponding god realm. (To get an idea of how long this is in human terms, one also needs to introduce into this equation the number of human years that correspond to a day in the respective god realm.) Thus one day in the Reviving Hell is equivalent to a lifetime in the realm of the Four Great Kings (in which one of their days is equivalent to fifty human years), and since the gods in that realm live five hundred years (in their own terms, that is), the beings in the Reviving Hell also live five hundred years, but Reviving Hell years in their case. In the Black Line Hell, one day is equivalent to a lifetime (one thousand years) in the Heaven of the Thirty-Three (in which one of their days is equivalent to one hundred human years), and Black Line beings there live one thousand Black Line years. And so on, the lifetimes in the Crushing, Screaming, Great Screaming, and Heat Hells being calculated in terms of the lifetimes in the Heaven Free of Conflict, the Joyous Realm, Enjoying Magical Creations, and Mastery over Others' Creations respectively. See also *The Words of My Perfect Teacher*, pp. 64 and 65.

68 Tib. *spangs pa*, more usually translated as "reject," but the verb is used here in a poetic sense to mean that the animals' being unsuitable vessels has prevented them from practicing virtue.

69 Tib. *dge ba nge 'byed cha mthun*: positive actions which accord with the wisdom of the path of seeing and are therefore distinct from those of ordinary beings.

70 An Asian palm tree, the tala tree.

71 *Introduction to the Middle Way*, VI, 71.

72 *The Way of the Bodhisattva*, V, 7 (last two lines) and 8 (first two lines).

73 Tib. *rten de la*, lit. "in that support," i.e., rebirth as an asura.

74 The "propelling action" is that which determines the particular kind of rebirth (in this case, as an asura). The "completing action" determines the conditions and circumstances experienced within that rebirth. The argument here is whether rebirth as an asura is determined by a negative propelling action (which would normally result in lower rebirth) but redeemed, as it were, by a positive completing action (which results in asuras having conditions similar to those of the gods); or whether a positive propelling action gives asuras a celestial rebirth which is spoiled by jealousy stemming from a negative completing action. See also *Treasury of Precious Qualities*, p. 50.

75 Other Buddhist authors have used the image of a beautiful woman's efforts as she panics at the prospect of being disfigured as a yardstick for endeavor in the practice, but here Nagarjuna advises us not to use such endeavor to stop samsara but rather to put our efforts into stopping being reborn.

76 Tib. *rnam byang phyogs*, refers to the last two truths, cessation and the path.

77 Jaina, Tib. *rgyal ba pa*, the founder of the Jain religion.

78 The wisdom referred to here is rather the wisdom gained through hearing and through reflection. Without these one does not have a subject on which to concentrate or meditate.

79 Friend of the Sun (Tib. *nyi ma'i gnyen*) is an epithet of the Buddha Shakyamuni.

80 In this case the Buddha's "perfect pronouncement" (Tib. *rab gsungs*) was to remain silent when asked about these fourteen points (Tib. *lung ma bstan pa bcu bzhi*).

81 Tib. *khyad gzhi*, the basis of predication.

82 Tib. *khyad chos*, the predicated properties.

83 It is important to bear in mind that, in this context, the word "exist" implies existence as a single, permanent, independent entity. Any reference to "nonex-

istence" is, therefore, used to invalidate such a notion, rather than imply a nihilistic void.

84 I.e., the predicated properties of a nonexistent basis of predication.

85 Also called "dependent arising." Kangyur Rinpoche gives a more detailed account of this in *Treasury of Precious Qualities*, pp. 85-93.

86 Unwavering action, Tib. *mi g.yo ba'i las*. An action, in the form of a profound state of meditative concentration (but devoid of bodhichitta), that invariably results in rebirth in the world of form or the formless world. The results of meritorious or positive actions (Tib. *bsod nams*) and nonmeritorious or negative actions (Tib. *bsod nam ma yin pa*), on the other hand, are dependent on conditions and therefore it is not possible to say with certainty exactly how they will ripen.

87 "Name" comprises the embryo's four aggregates of feeling, perception, conditioning factors, and consciousness; "form" is its fifth aggregate, and refers to the physical matter of the embryo.

88 One of the five crimes with immediate retribution, for example. See note 64.

89 Acharya Nagarjuna.

90 The upasaka's vows not to kill, steal, indulge in sexual misconduct, lie, and consume alcohol.

91 Bimbisara was the ruler of the Indian kingdom of Magadha during the Buddha's lifetime and an important patron of the Buddha and his Sangha. He was murdered by his son, Ajatashatru, who nevertheless later became an Arhat (see p. 91).

92 Lit. "all dharmas." Although this has been translated in its widest sense, the specific intent of this verse within the context that it was spoken is that all virtue or merit (one of the ten meanings of the word "dharma") originates in the mind.

93 Tib. *'khor gsum*, the concepts of subject, object, and action as truly existent.

Glossary

Abhidharma (Skt.), *chos mngon pa*. One of the Three Pitakas; the branch of the Buddha's teachings that deals mainly with psychology and logic.

Afflictive emotions, *nyon mongs pa*, Skt. *klesha*. Mental factors that influence thoughts and actions and produce suffering. The five principal afflictive emotions are attachment, aversion or hatred, bewilderment or ignorance, jealousy, and pride.

Aggregates. *See* Five aggregates.

Amitabha (Skt.), *'od dpag med*. The Buddha of Infinite Light.

Arhat (Skt.), *dgra bcom pa*. Lit. "one who has vanquished the enemy" (the enemy being afflictive emotions): a practitioner of the Basic or Fundamental Vehicle who has attained the cessation of suffering, i.e., nirvana, but not the Perfect Buddhahood of the Great Vehicle.

Arya (Skt.), *'phags pa*. A sublime being; in the Great Vehicle, a Bodhisattva on one of the ten Bodhisattva levels.

Asura (Skt.), *lha min*. Also called a demi-god or jealous god: a class of beings whose jealous nature spoils their enjoyment of their fortunate rebirth in the higher realms and involves them in constant conflict with the gods in the god realms.

Avalokiteshvara (Skt.), *spyan ras gzigs*. Chenrezig, the Bodhisattva of Compassion.

Avici (Skt.). The Sanskrit name of the Hell of Torment Unsurpassed. *See* Torment Unsurpassed.

Bhagavan (Skt.), *bcom ldan 'das*. An epithet of the Buddha, defined as he who has overcome (*bcom*) the four demons, who possesses (*ldan*) the six excellent qualities, and who does not dwell in either of the two extremes of samsara and nirvana but has gone beyond them (*'das*).

Bhikshu (Skt.), *dge slong*. A fully ordained monk.

Bhikshuni (Skt.), *dge slong ma*. A fully ordained nun.

Bodhisattva (Skt.), *byang chub sems dpa'*. A follower of the Great Vehicle whose aim is enlightenment for all beings.

Brahma (Skt.), *tshangs pa*. Lit. "pure": the name given to the principal god in the world of form.

Brahmin (Skt.). A member of the priestly caste in Indian society.

Capable One, *thub pa*, Skt. *Muni*. An epithet of the Buddha Shakyamuni, often translated as "Mighty One." He was called capable because, when he was a Bodhisattva and there was no one who had the courage to tame the most unfortunate beings with extremely gross views, afflictive emotions, and actions, he, our kind Teacher, was the only one, of all the 1,002 Buddhas of this Excellent Kalpa, who had the strength or capacity to vow to benefit them.

Childish beings, *byis pa*. Ordinary, ignorant beings who lack wisdom and are thus trapped in samsara.

Conqueror, *rgyal ba*, Skt. *Jina*. Also "Victorious One": a general epithet for a Buddha.

Dharma (Skt.), *chos*. The Buddha's doctrine, the teachings transmitted in the scriptures, and the qualities of realization attained through their practice. Note that the Sanskrit word *dharma* has ten principal meanings, including "anything that can be known." Vasubandhu defines the Dharma, in its Buddhist sense, as the "protective dharma" (*chos skyobs*): "It corrects (*'chos*) every one of the enemies, the afflictive emotions; and it protects (*skyobs*) us from the lower realms: these two characteristics are absent from other spiritual traditions."

Demon, *bdud*, Skt. *mara*. In the context of Buddhist meditation and practice, a demon is any factor that obstructs enlightenment. Four principal demons are described in the teachings: the demon of the aggregates, the demon of afflictive emotions, the demon of the Lord of Death, and the demon of the sons of the gods (or demon of distraction).

Eight great dangers (or fears), *'jigs pa chen po brgyad.* Those related to lions, elephants, fire, snakes, water, chains, robbers, and flesh eaters (harmful spirits and rakshasas).

Eight perfect qualities (of water), *yan lag brgyad.* Sweet, cool, soft, light (on the digestion), clear, without odor, not irritating to the throat, soothing on the stomach.

Elimination and realization, *spangs rtogs.* Eliminating (or getting rid of) all obscurations, and realizing the two kinds of knowledge of a Buddha (q.v.).

Five aggregates, *phung po lnga,* Skt. *pañchaskandha.* The five psycho-physical components into which a person can be analyzed and which together produce the illusion of a self. They are form, feeling, perception, conditioning factors, and consciousness.

Five causal aggregates, *nye bar len pa'i phung po lnga.* The five "tainted" aggregates produced by afflictive emotions and actions in a previous life and which will again produce further afflictive emotions and actions.

Five crimes with immediate retribution, *mtshams med lnga,* Skt. *pañcha-nantariya.* Also called five sins with immediate effect: (1) killing one's father, (2) killing one's mother, (3) killing an Arhat, (4) creating a split in the Sangha, and (5) malevolently causing a Buddha to bleed. Someone who has committed one of these five actions takes rebirth in the Hell of Torment Unsurpassed immediately after death, without going through the intermediate state.

Four concentrations, *bsam gtan bzhi,* Skt. *chaturdhyana.* The karmic result of practicing these four concentrations without integrating them with the path of enlightenment is that the meditator is reborn in one of the twelve ordinary realms of the four concentrations, in the world of form (see chart on pp. 184-185).

Four Noble Truths, *'phags pa'i bden pa bzhi,* Skt. *chaturaryasatya.* The truth of suffering, the truth of the origin of suffering, the truth of cessation, and the truth of the path. These constitute the foundation of Buddha Shakyamuni's doctrine, the first teaching that he gave (at Sarnath near Varanasi) after attaining enlightenment.

Four samadhis. *See* Four concentrations.

Gods, *lha*, Skt. *deva*. A class of beings who, as a result of accumulating positive actions in previous lives, experience immense happiness and comfort, and are therefore considered by non-Buddhists as the ideal state to which they should aspire. Those in the worlds of form and formlessness experience an extended form of the meditation they practiced (without the aim of achieving liberation from samsara) in their previous life. Gods like Indra in the world of desire, as a result of their merit, have a certain power to affect the lives of other beings and are therefore worshipped, for example, by Hindus.

Great Vehicle, *theg pa chen po*, Skt. *Mahayana*. The vehicle of the Bodhisattvas, referred to as great because it aims at full Buddhahood for the sake of all beings.

Higher realms, *mtho ris*. The gods' realms, the asuras' realm, and the human realm.

Indra (Skt.), *brgya byin*. The ruler of the Heaven of the Thirty-Three.

Jambudvipa (Skt.), *'dzam bu gling*. The southern continent according to Buddhist cosmology, the world in which we live.

Kamaloka (Skt.), *'dod khams*. The world of desire.

Klesha (Skt.). The Sanskrit term for afflictive emotions.

Lasting happiness, *'nges legs*. Lit. "certain good" or "ultimate excellence": the lasting happiness of liberation and omniscience (i.e., Buddhahood).

Lower realms, *ngan song*. The hells, the preta realm, and the animal realm.

Madhyamika (Skt.), *dbu ma*. The philosophical doctrine propounded by Nagarjuna and his followers, the Middle Way that avoids the extremes of existence and nonexistence.

Mahamuni (Skt.), *thub pa chen po*. The Great Capable One, an epithet of Buddha Shakyamuni.

Mahayana (Skt.). *See* Great Vehicle.

Mighty Victor, *rgyal dbang*. A Buddha who is victorious over the four demons.

Mount Meru, *ri rab*. Lit. "the supreme mountain": the four-sided mountain in the form of an inverted pyramid which is the center of our universe according to Buddhist cosmology.

Muni (Skt.), *thub pa*. *See* Capable One.

Naga (Skt.), *klu*. A serpentlike being (classed in the animal realm) living in the water or under the earth and endowed with magical powers and wealth. The most powerful ones have several heads.

Nirvana (Skt.), *mya ngan las 'das pa*. Lit. "beyond suffering": while this can be loosely understood as the goal of Buddhist practice, the opposite of samsara, it is important to realize that the term is understood differently by the different vehicles; the nirvana of the Basic Vehicle, the peace of cessation that an Arhat attains, is very different from a Buddha's nirvana, the state of perfect enlightenment that transcends both samsara and nirvana.

Non–Returner, *phyir mi 'ong ba*. In the context of the Basic Vehicle, a state of realization where one will no longer be reborn in the desire realm. It is the stage before the attainment of the level of Arhat. In the context of the Great Vehicle, a Bodhisattva Non-Returner is one who cannot return to a samsaric state of mind, though he may still manifest in samsara to benefit beings.

Parinirvana (Skt.), *mya ngan 'das*. The point at which an enlightened being leaves his or her earthly body.

Pitaka (Skt.), *sde snod*. Lit. "basket": a collection of scriptures, originally in the form of palm leaf folios stored in baskets. The Buddha's teachings are generally divided into three pitakas: Vinaya, Sutra, and Abhidharma.

Pratimoksha (Skt.), *so sor thar pa*. Lit. "individual liberation": the collective term for the different kinds of Buddhist ordination and their respective vows, as laid down in the Vinaya.

Pratyekabuddha (Skt.), *rang sangs rgyas*. A follower of the Basic Vehicle who attains liberation (the cessation of suffering) without the help of a spiritual teacher.

Preta (Skt.), *yi dvags*. Also known as hungry ghost or spirit: a class of beings whose attachment and miserliness in previous lives result in constant hunger and the frustration of their desires.

Profound insight, *lhag mthong*, Skt. *vipashyana*. The perception, through wisdom, of the true nature of things.

Samadhi (Skt.), *bsam gtan*. Meditative absorption of different degrees. Generally translated as "concentration."

Sangha (Skt.), *dge 'dun*. The community of Buddhist practitioners.

Samsara (Skt.), *'khor ba*. Lit. "wheel," and therefore also translated as "cyclic existence": the endless round of birth, death, and rebirth in which beings suffer as a result of their actions and afflictive emotions.

Sense of decency, *khrel yod*. Also "modesty," "consideration of others": to be ashamed because of what others might think if one commits negative actions. This is one of the seven noble riches (*'phags pa'i nor bdun*) listed in verse 32 of *Letter to a Friend*.

Sense of shame, *ngo tsha shes*. Also "conscientiousness," "honesty": to be ashamed of oneself if one commits negative actions. This is one of the seven noble riches (*'phags pa'i nor bdun*) listed in verse 32 of *Letter to a Friend*.

Seven precious attributes of royalty, *rin po che sna bdun*, Skt. *saptaratna*. Also called the "seven attributes of royalty" (*rgyal srid sna bdun*): the precious golden wheel, precious wish-fulfilling jewel, precious queen, precious minister, precious elephant, precious horse, and precious general.

Shastra (Skt.), *bstan bcos*. A commentary on the Buddha's teachings. The term shastra does not only apply to a commentary on one particular teaching (a named sutra, for example) but also includes works by both Indian and Tibetan masters that provide condensed or more accessible expositions of particular subjects.

Shramanera (Skt.), *dge tshul*. The first stage in monastic ordination. Shramaneras do not observe all the precepts of fully ordained bhikshus or bhikshunis, but it is incorrect to refer to them as "novices" in that many of them remain shramaneras throughout their lives without necessarily progressing to full ordination.

Shravaka (Skt.), *nyan thos*. Lit. "one who listens": one who follows the Basic Vehicle of the Buddha's teachings and aims to attain liberation for himself as an Arhat.

Six Ornaments, *rgyan drug*. The six great commentators on the Buddha's teachings: Nagarjuna, Aryadeva, Asanga, Vasubandhu, Dignaga, and Dharmakirti.

Six sense organs, *dbang po drug*, Skt. *sadindriya*. The eye, ear, nose, tongue, body, and mind.

Six transcendent perfections, *pha rol tu phyin pa drug*, Skt. *sadparamita*. Transcendent generosity, discipline, patience, diligence, concentration, and wisdom.

Sixteen great dangers (or fears), *'jigs pa chen po bcu drug*. Those related to (1) earth (earthquakes, landslides), (2) water (oceans, floods, drowning), (3) fire, (4) wind (cyclones), (5) lightning, (6) weapons, (7) imprisonment and the law, (8) robbers, (9) ghosts, (10) wild elephants, (11) lions, (12) poisonous snakes and food poisoning, (13) epidemics and disease, (14) untimely death, (15) poverty, and (16) not accomplishing one's wishes. Also listed as dangers and fears related to (1) obstacles created by *gyalpo* spirits, (2) celestial beings, (3) sicknesses caught from *sadag* spirits, (4) diseases such as leprosy, (5) famine, (6) war, (7) harm caused by *sadhus*, (8) harm caused by elemental spirits, (9) lightning, (10) frost and hail, (11) earthquakes, (12) fire, (13) water, (14) falling stars, (15) outer space, and (16) nightmares.

Sixteen subdivisions of the Four Noble Truths, *bden bzhi rnam pa bcu drug*. The four aspects of the truth of suffering—impermanent, unsatisfactory, empty, and not the self; those of the truth of origination—source, cause, intensely producing, and condition; those of the truth of cessation—cessation, pacification, goodness, and definitive; and those of the truth of the path—path, pertinent, effective, and conducive to release. (See *Treasury of Precious Qualities*, Appendix 3.)

Skandha (Skt.). *See* Five aggregates.

Source of good, *dge rtsa*. A positive or virtuous act that serves as a cause propelling one towards happy states.

Sovereign of the Conquerors, *gyal ba'i dbang po*. An epithet of the Buddha, one who is victorious over the four demons.

Sugata (Skt.), *bde bar gshegs pa*. Lit. "one who has gone to bliss": an epithet of a Buddha.

Sustained calm, *zhi gnas*, Skt. *shamatha*. The basis of all concentrations: a calm, undistracted state of unwavering concentration.

Sutra (Skt.), *mdo*. (1) A scripture containing the teachings of the Buddha; (2) the Sutra-pitaka (*mdo sde*), the one of the Three Pitakas that deals with meditation.

Tainted, *zag bcas*. Lit. "possessing the cause of downfall (*zag pa*)": tainted by afflictive emotions, or by concepts of subject, object, and action.

Tala (Skt.). An Asian palm tree, the palmyra.

Three Jewels, *dkon mchog gsum*, Skt. *Triratna*. The Buddha, Dharma, and Sangha.

Three Pitakas, *sde snod gsum*, Skt. *tripitaka*. *See* Pitaka.

Three Trainings, *bslabs pa gsum*, Skt. *trishiksa*. The threefold training in discipline, concentration, and wisdom.

Three vehicles, *theg pa gsum*, Skt. *triyana*. The vehicles of the Shravakas, Pratyekabuddhas, and Bodhisattvas.

Three worlds, *khams gsum*. The world of desire, the world of form, and the formless world (see chart on pp. 184-185). Alternatively (*'jig rten gsum, sa gsum, srid gsum*), the world of gods above the earth, that of humans on the earth, and that of the nagas under the earth.

Thus Gone, *de bzhin gshegs pa*, Skt. *Tathagata*. An epithet of a Buddha.

Thusness, *de bzhin nyid*, Skt. *tathata*. The absolute nature of things, emptiness, the absolute space free from elaboration.

Tirthika (Skt.), *mu stegs pa*. A proponent of extreme philosophical views such as nihilism and eternalism. This term is often used to imply non-Buddhist religious traditions in India.

Torment Unsurpassed, *mnar med*, Skt. *Avici*. The most terrible of the hells, also called the Hell of Ultimate Torment.

Two kinds of knowledge, *mkhyen gnyis*. Knowledge of the nature of things (*ji lta ba'i mkhyen pa*) and knowledge of all things in their multiplicity (*ji snyed pa'i mkhyen pa*).

Two kinds of no-self, *bdag med gnyis*. The no-self of the individual (*gang zag gi bdag med*) and the no-self of phenomena (*chos kyi bdag med*).

Universal monarch, *'khor los sgyur ba'i rgyal po*, Skt. *chakravartin*. An emperor who, with his golden, silver, copper, or iron wheel, has dominion over the beings of the four continents. Universal monarchs only appear in certain eras when the human life span is greater than eighty thousand years.

Upasaka (Skt.), *dge bsnyen*. A layman who has taken refuge in the Three Jewels and keeps one or more of the basic precepts.

Victorious One, *rgyal ba*, Skt. *Jina*. A general epithet for a Buddha.

Vinaya (Skt.), *'dul ba*. One of the Three Pitakas; the section of the Buddha's teaching that deals with discipline, and in particular with the vows of monastic ordination.

Yoga (Skt.), *rnal 'byor*. Lit. "union with the natural state": a term for spiritual practice.

Yogi (Skt.), *rnal 'byor pa*. A person practicing a spiritual path.

The Five Bodhisattva Paths and the Thirty-seven Elements

The Five Paths

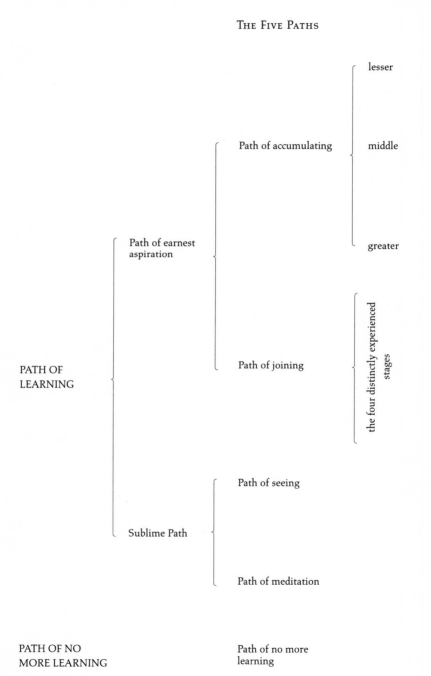

- PATH OF LEARNING
  - Path of earnest aspiration
    - Path of accumulating
      - lesser
      - middle
      - greater
    - Path of joining
      - the four distinctly experienced stages
  - Sublime Path
    - Path of seeing
    - Path of meditation
- PATH OF NO MORE LEARNING
  - Path of no more learning

Leading to Enlightenment

The 37 Elements of Enlightenment

	Four close mindfulnesses	1 mindfulness of the body 2 mindfulness of feelings 3 mindfulness of consciousness 4 mindfulness of mental objects
	Four genuine restraints	5 halting of negative thoughts not yet arisen 6 rejection of negative thoughts already arisen 7 solicitation of positive thoughts not yet arisen 8 preservation of positive thoughts already arisen
	Four bases of miraculous powers	9 concentration based on the power of the will 10 concentration based on endeavor 11 concentration based on one-pointed mindfulness 12 concentration based on analysis
warmth peak	Five powers	13 confidence 14 diligence 15 mindfulness 16 concentration 17 wisdom
acceptance supreme mundane level	Five irresistible forces	18 confidence 19 diligence 20 mindfulness 21 concentration 22 wisdom
1st Bodhisattva level	Seven elements leading to enlightenment	23 mindfulness 24 perfect discernment 25 diligence 26 joy 27 flexibility 28 concentration 29 evenness
2nd - 10th Bodhisattva levels	Eightfold Noble Path	30 right view 31 right thought 32 right speech 33 right conduct 34 right livelihood 35 right effort 36 right mindfulness 37 right concentration

The Three Worlds and the Six Realms

World of formlessness	Gods	Gods of the world of formlessness
World of form	Gods	The seventeen classes of gods of the world of form
World of desire	Gods	The six classes of gods of the world of desire
World of desire	Asuras	
World of desire	Humans	
World of desire	Animals	
World of desire	Pretas	
World of desire	Hells	

	The four formless realms at the peak of existence	Sphere of neither existence nor nonexistence Sphere of Utter Nothingness Sphere of Infinite Consciousness Sphere of Infinite Space
	The five pure abodes	Unsurpassed (Akanishtha) Good Vision Manifest Richness Without Distress Not Greater
The twelve ordinary realms of the four concentrations	Fourth concentration	Great Result Merit-Born Cloudless
	Third concentration	Flourishing Virtue Limitless Virtue Lesser Virtue
	Second concentration	Clear Light Measureless Light Dim Light
	First concentration	Great Pure Ones Priests of Brahma The Pure
	Gods of the four sky abodes	Mastery over Others' Creations Enjoying Magical Creations The Joyous Realm (Tushita) Heaven Free of Conflict (Yama)
	Gods on top of Mount Meru	Heaven of the Thirty-Three
	Gods on the steps of Mt. Meru	Four Great Kings
	Asuras	
	Humans of the four continents	
	Animals living in the depths Animals that live scattered in different places	
	Pretas who live collectively Pretas who move through space	
	The eight hot hells The neighboring hells The eight cold hells The ephemeral hells	

Bibliography

Works Quoted in the Text

Condensed Prajñaparamita Sutra – Sanchayagathaprajñaparamita-sutra, sdud pa.

Flower Garland of the Vinaya – Vinayapuspamala, dul ba me tog phreng rgyud; probably the *Vinayakarika* by Vishakadeva.

Introduction to the Middle Way – Madhyamakavatara, dbu ma la 'jug pa, by Chandrakirti (translated by the Padmakara Translation Group: *Introduction to the Middle Way*. Boston: Shambhala, 2002).

The Jewel Garland – Ratnavali, rin chen phreng ba, by Nagarjuna.

Lalitavistara Sutra – rgya cher rol pa; the *Sutra of the Great Play.*

The Ornament of the Mahayana Sutras – Mahayana-sutra-alankara-karika, mdo sde rgyan, by Maitreya-Asanga.

Rice Seedling Sutra – Arya-salistambha-nama-mahayana-sutra, sa lu ljang ba'i mdo; the sutra in which the Buddha describes dependent arising illustrated by the growth of rice.

Sutra of Interdependence – Arya-pratityasamutpada-nama-mahayana-sutra, rten 'brel gyi mdo.

Sutra of Sublime Dharma of Clear Recollection – Saddharmanu-smrityu-pasthana-sutra, dam pa'i chos dran pa nye bar bzhag pa'i mdo, also called the *Close Mindfulness Sutra.*

Sutra Requested by Surata – Arya-surata-pariprccha-nama-mahayana-sutra, 'phags pa des pas zhus pa zhes bya ba theg pa chen po'i mdo.

Treasury of the Abhidharma – Abhidharmakosha, chos mgnon mdzod, by Vasubandhu.

Verses on Interdependence – rten 'brel gyi tshigs su bcad pa.

The Way of the Bodhisattva – Bodhicharyavatara, byang chub sems dpa'i spyod pa la 'jug pa, by Shantideva (translated by the Padmakara Translation Group: *The Way of the Bodhisattva*. Boston: Shambhala, 1997).

Western-Language Sources

Beyer, Stephan, comp. *The Buddhist Experience: Sources and Interpretations*. Belmont: Wadsworth Publishing Company, 1974.

Dudjom Rinpoche. *Perfect Conduct: Ascertaining the Three Vows*. Boston: Wisdom Publications, 1996.

Kangyur Rinpoche, Longchen Yeshe Dorje. *Treasury of Precious Qualities*. Translated by the Padmakara Translation Group. Boston: Shambhala, 2001.

Nagarjuna and Lama Mipham. *Golden Zephyr: A Letter to a Friend*. Translated by Leslie Kawamura. Emeryville: Dharma Publishing, 1975.

Ngawang Khyenrab, Geshe. *La Lettre à un Ami du Supérieur Nagarjuna*. Translated by Georges Driessens, assisted by Michel Zaregradsky. Peymeinade: Editions Dharma, 1981.

Ngawang Pelzang, Khenpo. *A Guide to The Words of My Perfect Teacher*. Translated by Dipamkara and the Padmakara Translation Group. Boston: Shambhala, 2004.

Patrul Rinpoche. *The Words of My Perfect Teacher*. Translated by the Padmakara Translation Group. 2nd edition. Walnut Creek, Calif.: AltaMira Press, 1998; Boston: Shambhala, 1998.

Rendawa Zhö-nu Lo-drö. *Nagarjuna's Letter*. Translated by Geshe Lobsang Tharchin and Artemus B. Engle. Dharamsala: Library of Tibetan Works and Archives, 1975.

Tarthang Tulku, ed. *Guide to the Nyingma Edition of the sDe-dge bKa'-'gyur/bsTan-'gyur*. Berkeley: Dharma Publishing, 1983.

Tibetan Line Index

This line index has been prepared in Wylie transliteration to enable students of Tibetan to identify passages from the *Letter to a Friend* cited in other Tibetan texts. It should be borne in mind that minor differences (principally in the spelling of verbs and the use of connective particles) may be found between the root text as it appears in Kangyur Rinpoche's commentary and quotations used in other texts.

ka
kun gyi dge ba kun la yi rang zhing (119a)
kun tu chog shes mdzod cig chog mkhyen na (34c)
kun tu sbyor ba 'di gsum thar pa yi (51c)
kla klor skye dang glen zhing lkugs pa nyid (63d)
klu mchog rnams la mgo bo ji snyed pa (35c)
bkres skom grang dro ngal dang 'jigs pa yis (91c)
rkang pa'i reg pas nems par bde bzod pa (71a)
rkang lag rna ba sna gcod 'thob par 'gyur (72d)
skyabs med mgon med gnas med de slad du (58b)
skye 'di sdug bsngal sred pa zhes bgyi ba (114a)
skyes pa bud med dag la stsol bar bgyid (11d)
skye ba 'gags pas 'di kun 'gag par 'gyur (111d)
skye ba dpag tu med par lha mi yi (120a)
skye ba zhes bgyi mi khom skyon brgyad po (64b)
skye ba bzang po ma lags skye ba ni (103c)
skye ba bzlog pa'i slad du 'bad par mdzod (64d)
skye ba yod na mya ngan na rga dang (111a)
skye bo dgrar gyur pa dag bshes nyid dang (66b)
skye bo'i rjes su 'brangs ba'i khor ba pas (67c)
skyes bu dam pa bsten bgyi rgyal ba la (62c)
skyes bu dam pa la ni bsten pa dang (61b)
skyes bu rigs gzugs thos dang ldan rnams kyang (28a)
bskyed pa shin tu mi bzad bsten 'tshal lo (91d)
bskyed pa'i sdug bsngal rgyun chags mi 'chos pa (91b)

kha

kha cig kha ni khab kyi mig tsam la (92a)
kha cig lcags kyi mche ba ldan pa'i khyi (80a)
kha cig lcags kyi gsal shing rab 'bar ba (79c)
kha cig lcags las byas pa'i zangs chen du (82c)
kha cig til bzhin 'tshir te de bzhin du (78a)
kha cig mdag me 'bar ba'i tshogs su ni (82a)
kha cig lpags rus lus shing gcer bu ste (93a)
kha cig mu tig bal dang rus pa dang (90a)
kha cig mtshan zhing kha nas 'bar ba ste (93c)
kha cig sog les 'dra ste de bzhin gzhan (78c)
kha cig srin bu sbur pa sna tshogs dang (81a)
kha zas sman dang 'dra bar rigs pa yis (38a)
khu ba 'bar ba 'khrigs pa ldud par bgyid (79b)
khon du 'dzin pas 'khrug long rnams skyed de (16c)
khon 'dzin rnam spangs bde bar gnyid log 'gyur (16d)
khyim thabs brnyas bgyi jo mo lta bu dang (36b)
khyod kyi thugs su lta yang chud mod kyi (3b)
khyod kyis khro ba'i go skabs dbye mi bgyi (15b)
khyod kyis thugs dul mdzod cig bcom ldan gyis (117c)
khyod kyis bram ze dge slong lha dang ni (30a)
khyod kyis tshul khrims ma nyams mod mi dma' (7a)
khyod la de skad gdams pa gang lags de (118a)
khrag sogs mi gtsang ba yang mi rnyed de (94b)
khrims ni rgyu dang mi rgyu'i sa bzhin du (7c)
khro ba spangs pas phyir mi ldog pa nyid (15c)
mkhas rnams dang po dpa' rab lags par 'tshal (24d)
'khor gyi slad du'ang sdig pa mi bgyi ste (30c)
'khor ba chu shing snying po med pa las (58c)
'khor ba dag tu yang bran nyid du 'gyur (69d)
'khor ba dag na nges pa 'ga' ma mchis (66d)
'khor ba de 'dra lags pas lha mi dang (103a)
'khor ba'i btson rar 'jig rten 'di dag bcings (23d)
'khor lo chen po bzhi ni khyod la mnga' (61d)
'khor los sgyur ba nyid du gyur nas kyang (69c)
'khrungs nas na rga 'dod chags zhe sdang rnams (121a)

ga

gang gis 'di ni yang dag mthong ba des (112c)
gang dag chos mngon bgyis pa de dag kyang (116a)
gang dag dbang po drug yul rnams la ni (24a)
gang zhig sngon chad bag med gyur pa la (14a)

gang zhig mi ru skyes nas sdig pa dag (60c)
gang zag log par lta bas legs spyad kyang (47c)
gang zhig gser snod rin chen spras pa yis (60a)
gang la de gnyis yod pa srid pa yi (107c)
gang la pha dang ma dag mchod byed pa'i (9a)
gar dang phreng ba'i khyad par rnams spang zhing (10d)
gal te dge ba'i lhag ma 'ga' med na (101b)
gal te mtho ris thar pa mngon bzhed na (47a)
gus pas rtag tu bag dang bcas par mdzod (13d)
go 'phang mi rga mi 'chi zad mi 'tshal (105c)
gong ma brnyes par ma gyur de lta na'ang (40c)
gos la dri ma chags dang lus la ni (99c)
grags pa nyams par 'gyur ba'i de drug spangs (33d)
grong khyer sgo 'gegs lags par mkhyen par gyis (51d)
dga' dang shin tu spyangs dang ting 'dzin dang (106b)
dga' bo sor phreng mthong ldan bde byed bzhin (14d)
dge dang mi dge rnam lnga chen po ste (42c)
dge ba'i rtsa ba yangs la mkhyen par bgyi (43d)
dge ba'i bshes gnyen bsten pa tshangs par spyod (62a)
dge ba'i las lam bcu po lus dang ni (5a)
dge slong bram ze bkren dang bshes rnams la (6b)
dgra bcom tshul khrims rjes su byed pa yi (11a)
bgyid pa de ni ches rab blun pa lags (60d)
bgyis pa ci 'dra'ang rung ste mkhas pas mchod (2b)
bgrod pa gcig pa'i lam du nye bar bstan (54b)
mgon po sku tshe dpag tu med par mdzod (121d)
mgo'am gos la glo bur me shor na (104a)
mgron dang yab yum dag dang btsun mo dang (30b)
'gro ba nyams thag mang po rjes bzung ste (120d)
rgod dang 'gyod dang mnod sems rmugs pa dang (44a)
rgya mtsho gcig nas gnya' shing bu ga dang (59a)
rgya mtsho gnag rjes lta bur 'tshal bar bgyi (107d)
rgyags phyir ma lags bsnyem pa'i phyir ma lags (38c)
rgyan po 'gyed dang 'dus la lta ba dang (33a)
rgyal ba'i bka' med pa dang mtha' 'khob tu (63c)
rgyal ba'i dbang pos kim pa'i 'bras 'drar gsungs (23b)
rgyal bas snying la 'bab dang bden pa dang (18a)
rgyal bas sangs rgyas chos dang dge 'dun dang (4a)
rgyun mi 'chad par rab bsregs kha yang bgrad (82b)
sgrib pa lnga po 'di dag dge ba'i nor (44c)
sgrib pas bden pa mthong ba ma mchis so (102d)
brgya byin 'jig rten mchod 'os gyur nas ni (69a)

nga
ngag dang yid kyis rtag tu bsten bgyid cing (5b)
ngan skyugs 'phyag par bgyid pa de bas kyang (60b)
mngon pa'i nga rgyal 'dod chags zhe sdang dang (12b)
lnga stong dag dang khrir yang 'chir mi 'gyur (96d)
sngon chad med pa'i rngul 'byung zhes bgyi ba (99d)

ca
ci nas de rdul tsam yang ma mchis pa (88c)
cung zad cig bsdebs khyod kyis gsan par rigs (1d)
gcig pur nyi ma zla bas mi brdzi ba'i (76c)
gcig la gcig za shin tu mi bzad pa (89d)
bcing dang brdeg sogs sdug bsngal sna tshogs pa (89b)
lcags dang lcags kyu gdab pas btab ste bkol (90d)

cha
chang dang dus min zas la chags pa dang (10b)
chang dang mtshan mo rgyu ba ngan song du (33c)
chang rnams las ldog de bzhin dge ba yi (5c)
chu yi chu bur bas kyang mi rtag na (55b)
chung ngu'ang rku ba chom rkun lta bu yi (36c)
chung ma gsum po de yang rnam par spang (36d)
ches dkar nyid du ci ste mi bgyid lags (3d)
chos gzhan 'ga' yang mchis pa ma lags so (27d)
mchog ste chos 'dod rnams la tha ma lags (17d)
'chi 'pho'i sdug bsngal nyid ni de bas che (98b)
'chi ba zhi mdzad rgyal ba'i dbang po nyid brnyes nas (123b)
'chi ba'i dus la bab na sdig pa yi (31c)
'chi ba'i gnas su thub pas bka' stsal te (13b)

ja
ji ltar bde gshegs sku gzugs shing las kyang (2a)
ji ltar mdze can srin bus nyen pa ni (26a)
ji srid mi dge de zad ma gyur pa (87c)
'jig rten kun gyi rnal 'byor dbang mdzad nas (120b)
'jig rten mkhyen pa rnyed dang ma rnyed dang (29a)
'jig rten las 'das ming tsam zhi la mi bsnyengs pa (123c)
'jigs pa skyed par 'gyur na mi bzad pa'i (84c)
ljon shing 'bras bu med 'gyur 'di dag gis (95c)

nya
nyi ma zla ba nyid thob rang lus kyi (75a)
nyi ma'i gnyen gyis rab gsungs gang dag lags (108b)
nyid kyis legs par spyad pa rnam gsum yang (119b)
nyes par spyad pa'i las kyi zhags pa ni (96b)
nyon mongs nyam thag sems can tshogs kyi 'jigs skye dang (123a)
nyon mongs rag las so so'i skye bor bas (116d)
gnyid dang 'dod la 'dun dang the tshom ste (44b)
bsnyengs dang bral la ha cang mang ci 'tshal (117a)

ta
ta la'i yang thog bskams pa lta bu lags (93b)
ting 'dzin shes rab chos mchog lnga nyid de (45b)
gtum pos dbad cing lag pa gnam du bsgrengs (80b)
gter bzhin srog dang 'dra bar bsrung bgyi ste (22b)
gtong dang tshul khrims lha rjes dran pa drug (4b)
btang snyoms rtag tu yang dag sgom mdzod cig (40b)
btang snyoms 'di bdun byang chub yan lag ste (106c)
rtag tu mi brtan g.yo dang gang dag gcig (24b)
rtag dang mngon par zhen dang gnyen po med (42a)
rten cing 'brel bar 'byung 'di rgyal ba yi (112a)
lto ba ri yi gtos tsam bkres pas nyen (92b)
sta re mi bzad so rnon rnams kyis gshags (78d)
stan la mi dga' me tog phreng rnying dang (99b)
stobs dbang zhes bgyi rtse mor gyur pa'ang lags (45d)
brten nas rab tu mang pos zhi ba thob (62d)
bltas pa tsam gyis klung yang bskam par 'gyur (95d)
bstod smad ces bgyi 'jig rten chos brgyad po (29c)

tha
tha mar mi gtsang snying po ma mchis pa (56b)
thams cad rnam par smin pa mi bzad ldan (47d)
thar pa bdag la rag las 'di la ni (52a)
thal ba tsam yang lus par mi 'gyur na (57c)
thub pa chen po'i bka' ni snyan dgu zhig (3a)
thos dang tshul khrims bsam gtan ldan pa yis (52c)
mthun par gyur pa'i yul du gnas pa dang (61a)
mtho ris 'chi 'pho sbron bgyid 'chi ltas lnga (100a)
mtho ris na yang bde chen de dag gi (98a)
mtho ris bu mo'i nu ma sked pa la (70a)
mtho ris bu mos 'brongs shing dga' tshal dang (72a)

mthong bar bgyi slad rtag tu brtson par bgyi (115b)
'thob bgyid 'phags lam yan lag de brgyad lags (114d)
'thob par 'gyur ba sangs rgyas zhal gyis bzhes (15d)

da
dad dang brtson 'grus dag dang dran pa dang (45a)
dad dang tshul khrims thos dang gtong ba dang (32a)
dam chos brjod la bsten slad smad mi bgyid (2d)
dam chos spyod pas de 'bras mchis par mdzod (59d)
dal gyis 'bab pa lha yi bu mo ni (73a)
dud 'gro'i skye gnas na yang gsod pa dang (89a)
dus kyis bar du chod rnams dmyal ba yi (83b)
de ltar nyid kyi rtsal gyis 'bad par mdzod (88d)
de ltar 'di kun mi rtag bdag med de (58a)
de ltar sdug bsngal shin tu mi bzad lo (87a)
de ltar nongs par 'gyur 'tshal bsod nams ni (76a)
de ltar 'phags pa'i bden pa bzhi po dag (115a)
de ltar yang dang yang du sems pa ni (46c)
de ltar yi dvags rnams kyi sna tshogs pa'i (97a)
de ltar bsams nas ya rabs rnams kyis ni (98c)
de ltas gang la yon tan 'di gnyis ldan (28c)
de dag dang bral khom pa rnyed nas ni (64c)
de dag rnams la bsam par mi bgyi ste (108c)
de dag spang bgyi de yi lcags sgrog gis (23c)
de dag blo dang ldan yang 'gro ba yi (102c)
de dag bzlog phyir bgyi ba btang nas kyang (104b)
de dag la mchod grags par 'gyur ba dang (9c)
de dang 'dra ba'i yon tan ldan pa yi (27c)
de nas dge ba'i phung po 'di yis ni (119d)
de nas dbang med dud 'gro yi dvags dang (101c)
de ni bsgrims nas mngon par bsrung bgyi ste (54c)
de ni de yi kun 'byung rgya chen te (114b)
de ni yon tan gzhan dang bral yang mchod (28d)
de bas khyod kyi dge chos spel slad du (13c)
de bas dge ba spyod la brtson par bgyi (42d)
de bas ches mchog dgos pa gzhan ma mchis (104d)
de bas ches mang nyid cig btung 'tshal lo (67d)
de bzhin bdag gi snyan ngag 'di ngan yang (2c)
de bzhin sdig pa'i las ni chung ngu yang (43c)
de bzhin sdug bsngal kun gyi nang na ni (85c)
de bzhin gzhan dag khro chu bzhus ba yi (79a)

de bzhin shes rab gzhal med pha rol phyin (8b)
de yi rgyu ni skye bo 'jungs dga' ba (97c)
de yi gnyen po'i sgo nas rgyags mi 'gyur (46d)
de yi mod la mtshon bzhin mi gcod kyang (31b)
de yis blo ni zhi bar bgyid ma lags (108d)
de'i nang nyon mongs can la dang po ni (17c)
de las skye mched drug ste de las ni (109c)
de las byung ba'i sdug bsngal de snyed do (35d)
de las srid pa srid las skye ba lags (110d)
de srid srog dang bral bar mi 'gyur ro (87d)
des ni dmyal ba'i sdug bsngal chung ngu la'ang (86c)
des pa bdog mang ji ltar sdug bsngal ba (35a)
des pa 'dod pas phongs dang 'chi ba dang (65a)
don dam gzigs par bgyi slad dngos rnams la (27a)
dran dang bklags dang gzugs su bgyis rnams kyang (84b)
dran dang chos rab 'byed dang brtson 'grus dang (106a)
dran dang ting 'dzin ngag dang las mtha' dang (113b)
dran dang ldan par de dag bar du mnol (39d)
dran pa nyams pas chos kun 'jig par 'gyur (54d)
dran pa nye bar ma gzhag rnams kyis ni (48c)
dri nga ba dang sgo dgu dod pa dang (25b)
dri med ngo tsha shes dang khrel yod dang (32b)
gdug pa dug dang mtshon dang dgra bo dang (22c)
gdong mdzes gser gyi padma ldan zhugs nas (73b)
bdag gi yid yul min par mgo snyom mdzod (29d)
bdag nyid legs smon sngon yang bsod nams bgyis (61c)
bdag ni 'dis spyos 'dis btag pham par byas (16a)
bdag la gzugs mi gnas te de bzhin du (49c)
bde dags dga' ba nges par rab tu zhi mdzad do (122d)
bde dang mi bde snyan dang mi snyan dang (29b)
bde ba kun gyi nang na sred zad pa (85a)
bde ba don du me la kun bsten kyang (26b)
bde ba'i bdag por bgyid pa ji lta bar (85b)
bde bar gshegs pa'i gsung bsnyad las byung ba'i (1b)
bden pa rnam pa bzhi la 'bad pa mdzod (52d)
'dab ma ral gri 'dra tshal nags rnams kyis (72c)
'di 'gog pa ni thar pa lags te de (114c)
'di ltar bzod mtshungs dka' thub ma mchis pas (15a)
'di dag rgyas mdzod srid pa'i rgya mtsho yi (8c)
'di na nyin gcig mdung thung sum brgya yis (86a)
'di ni zhi bar bgyi slad bsgom par bgyi (113d)

'di yi nyes pa'i shas kyang gsan par mdzod (65d)
'di yis bdag gi nor 'phrog gyur to zhes (16b)
'di la mngon brtson mdzod cig 'di dag ni (45c)
'di las gang zhig spyod pa'i ngo bo de'i (118c)
'dod chags zhe sdang med par bsten bgyi ste (38b)
'dod pa chung rnams de lta ma lags te (35b)
'dod pa rnams ni phung khrol skyed pa ste (23a)
'dod pa rnams la chags pa'ang mkhyen par mdzod (26d)
'dod pas phongs dang 'chi dang 'jig sogs kyis (111b)
'dod spyod dga' dang bde dang sdug bsngal dag (41a)
rdo thal las bgyis dgung zla'i 'od kyis ni (3c)
sdig can dbugs 'byung 'gags pa tsam zhig gi (83a)
sdig pa'i las rnams spyad pa 'ga' yang ni (31a)
sdug bsngal rgyun mi 'chad pa brten 'tshal lo (74d)
sdug bsngal phung po shin tu che 'byung ste (111c)
sdug bsngal mi bzad phog snyam bgyid 'chal lo (71d)
sdug bsngal gzhal yas thos nas rnam stong du (83c)
sdug bsngal ro gcig thob pa gang lags pa (97b)
bsdus 'joms ngu 'bod mnar med la sogs pa'i (77c)

na
na rga 'chi sdug bral dang de bzhin du (46a)
na dang rga sogs sdug bsngal du ma yi (65b)
na tshod mthun par ma dang bu mo dang (21b)
nor rnams kun gyi nang na chog shes pa (34a)
nor mi bdog kyang yang dag 'byor ba lags (34d)
nor gzhan phal pa don ma mchis rtogs mdzod (32d)
gnam las babs pa ma lags lo tog bzhin (116b)
gnod pa du ma'i snod gyur lags mkhyen mdzod (103d)
mnar med me yi bud shing gyur pa yi (74c)
mnar med dmyal ba'i sdug bsngal rab mi bzad (85d)
mnal tshe'ang 'bras bu med par mi 'gyur bar (39c)
rnam par 'jig dengs myags par 'gyur ba ste (56c)
rnam par spangs pa'i bsam gtan bzhi po yis (41b)
rnam par mdzes tshal son par rtses nas slar (72b)
rnam smin nyams su myong na smos ci 'tshal (84d)
rnam shes de las ming dang gzugs rab 'byung (109b)
rnam gsum bka' stsal de las tha ma spang (18d)
rnam gsum mar me'i snang ba rab bzhes shig (76b)
snang nas snang ba'i mthar thug mun pa nas (19a)

pa
pags pas g.yogs dang rgyan yang logs shig gzigs (25d)
pang na dpal gnas khyim pa rnams kyis kyang (115c)
dpal la sdang phyir yid kyi sdug bsngal che (102b)
spyi'u tshugs 'bras kyi cung 'pheng bzhin du 'tshed (82d)

pha
pha ni bu nyid ma ni chung ma nyid (66a)
pha rol phyin pa rgyal ba'i dbang por mdzod (8d)
phan pa'i gdams ngag don po 'di lags te (117b)
phan tshun gdong du 'tshog cing mgren pa nas (94c)
phung po 'dod rgyal las min dus las min (50a)
phung po lhag ma bzhi yang stong rtogs bgyi (49d)
phyi nas bag dang ldan par gyur de yang (14b)
phyin ci log par lta dang the tshom ste (51b)
phyin ci log bzhir lta ba phung khrol ba (48d)
'phags pa spyan ras gzigs dbang spyod pa yis (120c)
'phrog pa'i chom rkun lags par mkhyen par mdzod (44d)

ba
bag yod bdud rtsi'i gnas te bag med pa (13a)
bar chad med par sdug bsngal bsten gyur pa (96a)
bas par dge slong gis kyang bgyi bar dka' (118b)
bud med gzhon nu'i lus ni logs shig tu (25a)
byams dang snying rje dag dang dga' ba dang (40a)
bye ba phrag brgyar nyams su myong yang ni (87b)
dbang gyur gang yin rigs kyi lha bzhin bkur (37d)
dbang thang che ba'i rgyags dge dgra bzhin gzigs (12d)
dbang phyug las min rgyu med can min te (50c)
dbang phyug lus gtogs dran pa bde gshegs kyis (54a)
dbang med gzhan dag lcags mchu rnon po dang (80c)
dbang med gzhan dag rdog pa lag pa dang (90c)
dbugs rngub dbugs 'byung gnyid kyi log pa las (55c)
'bar bas bsregs pa'i lus can 'di dag kyang (57b)
'byung gnas 'khor ba la ni skyo mdzad cing (65c)
'bras bu che lha rnams dang skal mnyam 'thob (41d)
lba ba byung ba smin pa'i rnag 'tshal lo (94d)
sbyin dang tshul khrims bzod brtson bsam gtan dang (8a)
sbyin pa tshul bzhin stsal bgyi pha rol tu (6c)
sbyin las gzhan pa'i gnyen mchog ma mchis so (6d)

sbrang rtsi me tog mi gtsang lta bu'i tshig (18c)
sbron par byed pa'i 'chi ltas rnams dang 'dra (100d)

ma
ma 'des ma sbags pa dag bsten par mdzod (7b)
ma smin ma smin par yang smin pa la (20c)
ma bzhin phan par 'dod dang bran mo bzhin (37c)
ma yi thug mtha' rgya shug tshig gu tsam (68c)
ma rig pa las las te de las ni (109a)
mal stan mtho la dga' dang glu dag dang (10c)
mi dge'i 'bras 'di rnams kyi sa bon ni (88a)
mi 'gres nongs pa mi mnga'i go 'phang brnyes par mdzod (123d)
mi mchog khyod kyis thugs ni dbugs dbyung mdzod (58d)
mi 'jigs gang lags rdo rje'i rang bzhin no (83d)
mi nyid ches thob dka' bas mi dbang gis (59c)
mi rtag bdag med mi gtsang rig par bgyi (48b)
mi ni yang dag nyid du mi bde zhing (48a)
mi ni a mra'i 'bras bzhin ma smin la (20a)
mi gtsang kun snod 'dra ba dgang dka' dang (25c)
mi gtsang gyi nar bor ba chung zad kyang (92c)
mi gtsang nyid du yang dag bsam par bgyi (21d)
mi shes las dang sred las byung rig mdzod (50d)
mun nag mtha' dag nang du 'jug 'tshal lo (76d)
mun nas snang ba'i mthar thug gang zag ni (19c)
mun pa'i mthar thug snang nas mun mthar thug (19b)
me bzhin 'dod pa'i bde la yid 'byung mdzod (22d)
mya ngan 'das thob bgyid pa'i dge tshogs lags (106d)
mya ngan 'das zhi dul ba dri med pa'i (105b)
dmyal ba rnams su rtag tu sdug bsngal 'gyur (77d)
dmyal ba bris pa mthong dang thos pa dang (84a)
dmyal ba yi dvags 'dud 'gro rnams dag tu (103b)
dmyal ba'i rnam smin skal nod 'ga' ma mchis (30d)
dmyal bar 'thag gcod dbad pa'i 'khrul 'khor gyi (70c)
dmyal bar gnas pa gang yang rung bar 'gyur (101d)
smad rigs 'ga' ni rnag dang phyi sa dang (94a)
smin pa dang 'dra smin la ma smin 'dra (20b)
smin par snang zhes bgyi ba 'drar rtogs mdzod (20d)

tsha
tshangs nyid chags bral bde ba thob nas slar (74b)
tshangs pa'i 'jig rten bde ba thob par 'gyur (40d)

ya
yan lag brgyad po 'di dag dang ldan na (11b)
yang dag rtog nyid lam gyi yan lag brgyad (113c)
yang dag lta dang 'tsho dang rtsol ba dang (113a)
yang dag lta la goms pa nyid du mdzod (47b)
yang sos thig nag rab tu tsha ba dang (77b)
yang srid med par bgyi slad 'bad 'tshal te (104c)
yi dvags nyid dang dmyal bar skye ba dang (63b)
yi dvags na yang 'dod pas phongs pa yis (91a)
yi dvags rnams la sos ka'i dus su ni (95a)
yongs su rdzogs par thub pas gsungs de'i phyir (62b)
yon tan kun gyi gzhi rten lags par gsungs (7d)
yon tan bsten pas sku tshe don yod mdzod (118d)
yon tan gtso ldan gzhi las byung ba'i las (42b)
yon tan tshogs kyi rjes su dran par bgyid (4d)
yon tan rang bzhin dge 'os bdag gis ni (1a)
g.yul ngor dgra tshogs las rgyal de dag las (24c)
g.yo ba'i sems ni thos mtshungs bu lta bur (22a)

ra
rang gi lag pa brkyang ba'ang mi mthong 'gyur (75d)
rang bzhin dgra 'brel gshed ma lta bu dang (36a)
rang bzhin las min ngo bo nyid las min (50b)
rab mchog lags par lha mi'i ston pas gsungs (34b)
rab tu bka' stsal de dag so so yi (4c)
rab tu drag btab bsdug bsngal gang lags pa (86b)
ri mor bris pa de 'drar rig par bgyi (17b)
rigs dang gzugs dang thos pa lang tsho dang (12c)
rigs de tshangs bcas slob dpon bcas pa'ang lags (9b)
rigs pa'i bdag nyid nyin par mtha' dag dang (39a)
ril bur bgrangs kyang sa yis lang mi 'gyur (68d)
rus sbal phrad pa bas kyang dud 'gro las (59b)
re re'i bdag nyid rus pa'i phung po ni (68a)
re res rgya mtsho bzhi bas lhag pa yi (67a)
reg na mi bzang rma srol cher 'byin pas (81c)
reg pa kun tu 'byung bar thub pas gsungs (109d)
reg pa shin tu mi bzad bsten 'tshal lo (70d)
reg pa las ni tshor ba kun 'byung ste (110a)
reg pa'i bde ba yun ring myong nas slar (70b)
ro bsgyur nus kyi gangga'i klung min ltar (43b)

la
lan tshva srang 'gas chu ni nyung ngu zhig (43a)
las kyi dbang gis phyir yang sa steng lhung (69b)
las kyi 'bras bu gang lags mngon pa 'gyur (31d)
las ni bdag gi byas las ma 'das zhes (46b)
lung ma bstan pa bcu bzhi 'jig rten na (108a)
lus kyi kha dog mi sdug 'gyur ba dang (99a)
lus ngag yid kyi nyes spyad khyod kyis ni (88b)
lus mtha' thal ba mthar skam mthar 'drul zhing (56a)
le lo sdig pa'i grogs la brten pa dang (33b)
log par lta ba 'dzin dang dud 'gro dang (63a)
log par smra ldan skyes bu rnams kyi ni (18b)
longs spyod g.yo ba snying po med mkhyen nas (6a)

sha
sha dang lpags pa'i ched du 'chi bar 'gyur (90b)
sha sbrang sbrang ma nag po khri phrag dag (81b)
shin tu nyams chung mi lta smos ci 'tshal (57d)
shes pas nyon mongs chu bo las brgal gyi (115d)
shes rab nor bdun lags par thub pas gsungs (32c)
shes rab med par bsam gtan yod min te (107a)
shes rab tshul khrims gtong 'byung grags chen dri ma med (122a)
shes rab tshul khrims bral ba bkur ma lags (28b)

sa
sa chu me rlung nyi zla bral thob mdzod (105d)
sa steng mi rnams 'chi bar 'gyur ba dag (100c)
sa dang lhun po rgya mtsho nyi ma bdun (57a)
sa rum nas 'thon ma lags de dag sngon (116c)
sa la mi dang mtho ris lha ni na chung mchog (122c)
sangs rgyas nyid thob bgyi slad yongs bsngos nas (119c)
sangs rgyas de nyid rig pa rnam mchog mthong (112d)
sad khom gang lags de ni ngo mtshar che (55d)
sen mo mi bzad ldan pa'i khva rnams 'thog (80d)
sems can nyes par spyad pa spyod rnams la (77a)
sems ni chu dang sa dang rdo ba la (17a)
sems ni chos kyi rtsa ba lags par gsungs (117d)
ser sna 'phags min lags par sangs rgyas gsungs (97d)
ser sna g.yo sgyu chags dang snyom las dang (12a)
so sor 'gyes chos can du mkhyen par mdzod (56d)
sra bas bcings pa'i lus can kha cig lo (96c)

sring mo lta bur rjes mthun gang yin dang (37a)
sring mo'i 'du shes bskyed bgyi chags gyur na (21c)
sred las len pa skye bar 'gyur ba ste (110c)
slad ma la yang mtho ris thob 'gyur lags (9d)
slar yang mun nag smag tu phyin gyur nas (75c)
slar yang me mur ro myags rgyu ba yi (71c)
slar yang dmyal ba'i chu bo rab med par (73c)
gsung gi mdzod kyi gces pa zab mo ste (112b)
gsum po 'di nang yang dag 'du bar 'gyur (53d)
gso spyong 'dod spyod lha lus yid 'ong ba (11c)
bsam gtan med par yang ni shes rab med (107b)
bsal te sangs rgyas zhing du bcom ldan 'das (121b)
bsod nams 'dun slad 'phags pa'i dbyangs 'di dag (1c)
bslab pa brgya rtsa lnga bcu lhag gcig ste (53c)

ha
lha min dag na'ang rang bzhin gyis lha yi (102a)
lha yi 'jig rten dag nas 'phos pa la (101a)
lha yul 'dod bde shin tu chen po dang (74a)
lha yul nam mkha' dang ni sa steng rgyas bdzad nas (122b)
lha yul gnas pa'i lha rnams la 'byung ste (100b)
lhag pa'i tshul khrims lhag pa'i shes rab dang (53a)
lhag pa'i sems la rtag tu bslab par bgyi (53b)
lhun po mnyam pa snyed cig 'das gyur te (68b)
lhun po'i spo la yun ring gnas nas ni (71b)

General Index

action(s),
  classified according to their result, 127-128, 170n64
  negative, 99-100, 120, 133
    the seven, 116, 169n52
    the ten, 85-86
      positive, 19, 85-86, 107
  positive and negative, 88
    five great kinds of, 107
  propelling and completing, 138-139, 171n74
affliction, 117, 169n54
aggregates, the, 105, 112-115, 119, 140, 143, 145, 154, 167n33, 168n45, 172n87
Amitabha, 153
anger, 23, 92-93, 166n20
Angulimala, 90, 91, 166n16
animals, sufferings of, 133-134, 170n68. *See chart* 184-185
arrogance, 89, 110-111
Asanga, 14, 139
asuras, 138-139, 171nn73, 74. *See chart* 184-185
attachment, 22, 87, 89, 96
  getting rid of, 97, 103-104
Avalokiteshvara. *See* Chenrezig

Bimbisara, 150, 172n91
birth,
  and rebirth, 85, 111, 122, 139, 152, 166n8
  human, a, 21, 119-120, 169n60. *See chart* 184-185
Bodhicharyavatara. See *Way of the Bodhisattva, The*
bounteousness, 85, 86, 101

Brahma, 87, 127, 167n37
Buddhahood, 21, 153-154

carefulness and carelessness, 89-90
celestial beings. *See* asuras; gods
Chandrakirti, 20
Chenrezig (Avalokiteshvara), 152
concentration(s), 20, 87, 95-109
  five hindrances to, 108-109
  the four, 20, 106, 167n35. *See chart* 184-185
  superior, 116, 169n53
Condensed Prajñaparamita Sutra, 136-137
confidence, 110. *See also* faith
contentment, 102, 167n32
craving pleasure, 108, 109. *See also* desire

Darshaka, 90, 91
dedication, 152
  results of, 152-153
dependent arising. *See* interdependence
desire, 22, 23, 89, 95-98
  world of, 127. *See chart* 184-185
  See also craving pleasure
Devadatta, 91, 113
diligence, 87, 94, 110, 115, 141
discipline, 85, 86-87, 88-89
  superior, 116, 140
dullness, 108, 109

eight defective states, the, 122
eight ordinary concerns, the, 98-99
eight unfavorable conditions, the, 122
encouragement, 150-151

Index of Figurative Elements and Images

The Padmakara Translation Group

The Padmakara Translation Group is devoted to the accurate and literary translation of Tibetan texts and spoken material into Western languages by trained Western translators, under the guidance of authoritative Tibetan scholars, principally Taklung Tsetrul Pema Wangyal Rinpoche and Jigme Khyentse Rinpoche, in a context of sustained study and discussion.

Translations into English

The Excellent Path of Enlightenment, Dilgo Khyentse, Editions Padmakara, 1987; Snow Lion Publications, 1996.

The Wish-Fulfilling Jewel, Dilgo Khyentse, Shambhala, 1988.

Dilgo Khyentse Rinpoche, Editions Padmakara, 1990.

Enlightened Courage, Dilgo Khyentse, Editions Padmakara, 1992; Snow Lion Publications, 1994.

The Heart Treasure of the Enlightened Ones, Dilgo Khyentse and Patrul Rinpoche, Shambhala, 1992.

A Flash of Lightning in the Dark of Night, the Dalai Lama, Shambhala, 1993.

Wisdom: Two Buddhist Commentaries, Khenchen Kunzang Pelden and Minyak Kunzang Sönam, Editions Padmakara, 1993, 1999.

The Words of My Perfect Teacher, Patrul Rinpoche, International Sacred Literature Trust—HarperCollins, 1994; 2nd edition, AltaMira Press, 1998; Shambhala, 1998.

The Life of Shabkar: Autobiography of a Tibetan Yogi, SUNY Press, 1994; Snow Lion Publications, 2001.

Journey to Enlightenment, Matthieu Ricard, Aperture, 1996.

The Way of the Bodhisattva (Bodhicharyavatara), Shantideva, Shambhala, 1997.

Lady of the Lotus-Born, Gyalwa Changchub and Namkhai Nyingpo, Shambhala, 1999.

Treasury of Precious Qualities, Longchen Yeshe Dorje, Kangyur Rinpoche, Shambhala, 2001.

Counsels from My Heart, Dudjom Rinpoche, Shambhala, 2001.

Introduction to the Middle Way, Chandrakirti and Mipham Rinpoche, Shambhala, 2002.

Food of Bodhisattvas, Shabkar Tsokdruk Rangdrol, Shambhala, 2004.

A Guide to The Words of My Perfect Teacher, Khenpo Ngawang Pelzang, (transl. with Dipamkara), Shambhala, 2004.

The Hundred Verses of Advice, Dilgo Khyentse and Padampa Sangye, Shambhala, 2005.

The Adornment of the Middle Way, Shantarakshita and Mipham Rinpoche, Shambhala, 2005.